THE ETHICAL CAPITALIST

Julian Richer established Richer Sounds in 1978. The business now turns over in excess of £200 million a year, and Richer Sounds has won the prestigious *Which?* Best Retailer award (2010, 2011 and 2015). In 2011 Richer Sounds was granted a Royal Warrant by HRH The Prince of Wales for the supply of consumer electronic products to the Royal Household. The first shop to be opened, near London Bridge, has for over 20 years been listed in *Guinness World Records* as achieving the highest sales per square foot of any retail outlet in the world. Fifteen per cent of the company's profits are donated to charitable causes (over 400 of them in 2017). In addition to his commercial activities, Julian Richer is the founder and a trustee of Acts 435, set up to help those in need, and in 2013 he established ASB Help, which works with victims of anti-social behaviour. In 2017 he founded TaxWatch to investigate and expose tax abuses, and in 2020 he launched both Zero Hours Justice to campaign against the unfairness of zero hours contracts and the Good Business Charter to encourage responsible capitalism. He lives in Yorkshire.

Also by Julian Richer:

The Richer Way
Richer on Leadership

Julian Richer

THE ETHICAL CAPITALIST

How to Make Business Work Better for Society

3 5 7 9 10 8 6 4

Random House Business
20 Vauxhall Bridge Road
London SW1V 2SA

Random House Business is part of the Penguin Random House
group of companies whose addresses can be found
at global.penguinrandomhouse.com.

Penguin
Random House
UK

First published by Random House Business Books in 2018
This edition published by Random House Business Books in 2019

www.penguin.co.uk

A CIP catalogue record for this book is available from the British Library.

ISBN 9781847942210

Printed and bound in Great Britain by Clays Ltd, Elcograf S.p.A.

The authorised representative in the EEA is Penguin Random House
Ireland, Morrison Chambers, 32 Nassau Street, Dublin D02 YH68.

Penguin Random House is committed to a sustainable future
for our business, our readers and our planet. This book is
made from Forest Stewardship Council® certified paper.

FSC
www.fsc.org

MIX
Paper from
responsible sources
FSC® C018179

To my wife Rosie

CONTENTS

PRELIMINARY NOTE

I'M VERY AWARE that anyone who writes a book with the word 'ethical' in the title is asking for trouble. So let me admit at the outset that I am deeply flawed!

I'm also aware that it must seem contradictory for me to be critical of many aspects of capitalism when I myself have done so well out of it.

But I do believe there are better ways of doing things, and I hope my own shortcomings don't get in the way of letting me put across views that I strongly hold.

PREFACE

WITH MORE THAN forty enjoyable and challenging years in business under my belt, I am proud to call myself an entrepreneur. But as I look around I am increasingly angered by what I see elsewhere: disreputable people (mostly men) running their companies in a way that involves taking as much as they can from society and then sneaking their profits out of the country. No doubt they think they're clever.

I'd like to think that while they are abhorrent, they are also in a minority. Nevertheless they grab the headlines and give other entrepreneurs and traders a bad name. Furthermore, their activities often seem to be treated – and forgiven – as though they are an inevitable by-product of the capitalist way of doing things.

I don't accept this. In my view it's possible to run a company both successfully and ethically. In fact, I'd go further. My own experiences in the business world suggest that an ethical approach, far from being a potential barrier to profits, is actually the secret to success.

My retail chain, Richer Sounds, has survived and thrived for more than forty years, through three recessions and the onslaught of internet selling. We may not be a huge global company, but we know what it means to fight for every pound in a highly competitive marketplace that has gone through immense technological change. In the early 1980s, when we sold the hi-fi separates we were so passionate about, we could not have imagined the way people acquire and listen to music these days (nor the size of TV screens now!). The success and resilience of Richer Sounds has only been possible, I believe, because we try to act in an ethical way.

What do I mean by ethical? I mean treating staff, customers and suppliers honestly, openly and respectfully. I mean taking responsibility for our actions, owning up when things go wrong and setting out to put them right. I mean seeing ourselves as an integral part of society and paying our dues – and taxes – accordingly. By following this approach I believe we create a virtuous circle for ourselves: not only can we sleep better at night, but a fair and honest approach to customers and staff leads to a huge competitive advantage that in turn reinforces the need to be fair and honest.

To my mind, ethical business is about two inter-related questions. The first is, what are the whys and wherefores of operating an ethical organisation? The second is, how can we, as a society, ensure that capitalism more generally is ethically controlled?

Let me say at the outset that I am an absolute believer in capitalism. I think it is the only economic system humans have so far come up with that offers the real promise of personal prosperity and well-being. However, I am also deeply aware of its short-comings. People sometimes argue that either you are a capitalist, in which case you accept its drawbacks, or you're not. I don't believe that at all.

INTRODUCTION

MY INVOLVEMENT IN the world of business began early on. When I was fourteen, I bought a Bang & Olufsen turntable for £10, cleaned it up and promptly sold it for £22. The profit I made – equal to a term's pocket money in 1973 – was enough to get me hooked. By the time I was seventeen I was hiring a large white Mercedes every Tuesday and Thursday afternoon to ferry me around Bristol as I bought up and then resold stereos that local shops had taken in part-exchange during the hi-fi separates boom of the early 1970s. From there it was only a short step to getting a hi-fi shop of my own, just two years later when I was nineteen, in tiny premises at London Bridge.

Arguably, my first encounter with the world of ethical business came even earlier than my first business deal. As a young child I listened as my parents recalled how they met when they were both trainee managers at the Kilburn branch of Marks and

Spencer and as they described what the company had been like to work for. In those days, they explained, M & S was a very paternalistic organisation. When the chairman visited a branch he might have arrived in a chauffeur-driven limousine but the first thing he did was to check the staff loos for cleanliness and the canteen for the quality of the hot food on offer. My parents always talked about him with respect. I therefore grew up with the idea that a company should care about its employees and that if it did the employees in turn would be loyal to the company. Later, when I went to Clifton College, I was to be hugely inspired by my housemaster Ernest Polack, whose idea of a holiday was to go to South Africa to demonstrate against apartheid (and to get beaten up for his troubles). He instilled in me a passionate belief in equality and human rights, just as many years later my wife was to inspire me with her deeply held Christian beliefs and values.

A love of buying and selling has stayed with me ever since I sold that first turntable. And there's no doubt that the profit motive has, too. I've always been driven by a desire to make money, especially in the early years. But the notion that how you treat people is central to how you conduct business stayed with me as I built my company and learnt from my mistakes.

What really transformed my thinking was reading Tom Peters' and Robert Waterman's classic business text *In Search of Excellence*, which I first encountered over thirty years ago. The authors identified various factors that they believed made companies successful. Key among them were how they treated their employees and customers ('Far too many managers have lost sight of the basics, in our opinion,' they argued; 'quick action, service to customers, practical innovation, and the fact that you can't get any of these without virtually everyone's commitment'). I began to apply *In Search of Excellence* ideas to my own business and found they really produced results. I also got to test them in a very different company environment in the early 1990s when Archie Norman, newly arrived at Asda, invited me to introduce my approach in their superstores. Asda had a completely different staff demographic from our own, and was a far larger enterprise, with 75,000 employees at the time, but we proved that the things that Richer Sounds did to motivate colleagues and boost productivity worked there, too. People are basically the same wherever they're working – old, young, female, male, part-time, full-time: they all want to be valued and treated well and they all have a lot to contribute, given the chance.

It's a simple formula. The key to increased sales is good value products alongside good customer service, and the key to the latter is highly motivated, highly trained staff (or, rather, colleagues, as we refer to them at Richer Sounds). I set out my principles in a book, *The Richer Way*, showing how they worked for us, and arguing that they could (and, I absolutely believe, still can, twenty-five years later) be applied in any organisation, including those in the public sector.

Of course businesses need to be profitable, or else they will go bust and jobs will be lost. But the pursuit of profit before everything is not the key to business success. If profits are only gained by paying employees and suppliers the bare minimum and giving customers a bad deal, in the long run the business won't thrive. Customers, and suppliers, will have no loyalty to the brand and will just as quickly turn to a competitor. Employees who are badly treated will never give their best: productivity will be poor and profits will suffer, and the good people will leave.

By the same token, the pursuit of high ethical standards serves to make a business stronger and more competitive. It should not therefore be treated as a nice optional add-on when times are good. It should be the central core of the enterprise, the motivating force that will help pull it through when times are bad.

In calling this book *The Ethical Capitalist*, I recognise that, on the whole, business people don't like to be called capitalists. The terms 'entrepreneurs' or 'wealth creators' sound so much nicer and more admirable. But you can't get away from the fact that it is the capitalist set-up in which we operate that enables us to make our money.

For many, an economic system based on the private ownership of the means of production and the private profit that arises from this ownership is inherently wrong. It places an emphasis on what people can afford rather than what they necessarily need. And because money and power are linked, it gives disproportionate influence to the rich and can leave the poor without a voice. I completely acknowledge these dangers, but I also believe that capitalism has benefits that can go well beyond simply enriching owners and shareholders. For a start, it encourages hard work. I didn't make much effort at school because I didn't see any advantage in it. The minute I had my first shop, at nineteen, I was like a greyhound out of the trap. There was nothing stopping me – I was working seven days a week and loving it. Since then, I've learned to pace myself and achieve a far better work-life balance, but entrepreneurial energy is a real force. Anyone running their own business knows how motivating it is.

That desire to succeed and make money spurs people to source, produce and sell the goods and services that others want to buy, and they will go to the nth degree to achieve this. They will also constantly innovate and make improvements (assuming that the market is a healthy one and not rigged). Admittedly, they profit from this. But consumers gain, too.

By contrast, in societies where free enterprise is stifled, where the system is controlled by the state, or where markets are dominated by corrupt monopolies or oligopolies, the consumer has tended to suffer. Choice dwindles. The quality of products and services sinks lower and lower.

The desire to make money leads to job creation. You can earn a certain amount as an individual maker of widgets, but you will make more if you can employ others to produce them for you. That shift up from sole trader to employer makes all the difference to profitability. And once you become part of a manufacturing or supply chain you indirectly support a whole range of other jobs, from distributors to accountants. You also become a significant contributor to the country as a whole, through the taxes that you and your staff should pay (a topic to which I will return later). After all, it's the taxes that private concerns and employees hand over to the government that fund nurses, firefighters and teachers, and others in the vital public service sector.

To my mind, perhaps the best illustration of the benefits of capitalism is to see the impact it has on local economies and communities. A high street crammed with shops and businesses is a bustling, vibrant place. When those enterprises go, and their premises are boarded up, people talk about an area having no 'life' to it. It quickly goes into a downward spiral. Trade and business can create 'life' – busy-ness, variety, purpose.

I've focused on the profit motive, but I think it would be wrong to say that it's the only motive to be found in capitalism. Business leaders are driven by a complex range of impulses. The desire to make money is certainly one. But there is also the satisfaction of being their own boss, of providing jobs, of having a good reputation, of creating attractive products or delivering a professional service. These are all strong drivers. The same goes for their employees. In a good company, what motivates people to turn up for work each day is much more than the amount in their wage packet. Their job satisfaction is much more likely to derive from getting on well with their colleagues, feeling part of a team and seeing customers happy.

So capitalism can work in many ways that are good for people and for society. But I accept that, as with any political and economic system – particularly one founded on individual profit and, dare I say it, greed – it also poses challenges and threats.

At its worst, it leads to the exploitation of employees, who can end up being treated as just another factor of production. Too many businesses today have not progressed much beyond the nineteenth-century mill owners who saw their employees merely as 'hands'. Years of pressure, mostly by trades unions, may have resulted in protection and rights for workers in developed countries, but the worst capitalists will always try to find ways round that protection.

Capitalism can also lead to huge social inequality. Karl Marx observed 150 years ago: 'Accumulation of wealth at one pole is, ... at the same time, accumulation of misery ... at the opposite pole.' Some argue that wealth creation at one end automatically leads to wealth creation at the other end – the so-called 'trickle-down effect'. The evidence, though, doesn't support this. In fact what seems to happen is that, unless controlled in some way, wealth becomes ever more concentrated in the hands of a small elite who proceed to get richer and richer, while the remainder of the population is left ever further behind. In the UK wealth inequality has been growing steadily since the 1980s. Today, the richest 10 per cent of the population have around 30 per cent of the nation's income, while the poorest 10 per cent get around 1 per cent share. The distribution of wealth is even more unequal: at present more than half the personal wealth in the UK is held by only 10 per cent of households. And the differential is getting worse.

Given that we are all very different from one another, a degree of inequality is inevitable. It is also arguably desirable. Certainly, I would not have worked so hard to create my business if I had not started off with very little money and been intent on having more. Most of us put in the hours in order to improve life for ourselves and our family. We want to 'get on'. But if people are locked into poverty, and see opportunities concentrated in the hands of a small elite, the very real danger is that they will give up. Why should they try to improve their lot if it's so hard to do so? And why should they support a society that is doing so little to support them? The point that Thomas Piketty makes in his seminal book *Capital in the Twenty-first Century* – that increasing inequalities in wealth cause social and economic instability – is, to my mind, a thoroughly convincing one

Once this happens, the lives of the rich and the poor become self-reinforcing. The poor become powerless, trapped in a vicious circle of deprivation. The rich become richer, not least because their increasing power and influence allows them to buy such hefty privileges as – not least – exemption from taxation. As I discuss later, wealth and political clout are intimately connected.

The irony is that social inequality is actually bad for capitalism. For businesses to thrive, we need people to be in secure jobs and decent homes, able to spend confidently. They should not be condemned to a low-wage economy such as the one we have in the UK, where the Child Poverty Action Group talks of one in four children growing up in poverty, where food-banks have become ever more necessary, and where, according to the National Audit Office, there was a 60 per cent increase in the number of homeless house-holds between 2011 and 2016. In a healthy economy, money needs to be widely distributed and circulating, not siphoned off to unproductive tax havens. Furthermore, social inequality is expensive. All the evidence suggests that it creates problems in society that are enormously expensive to fix. A country such as the UK, which has a relatively wide gap between rich and poor, also has higher levels of crime, obesity, illiteracy and other health and social problems.

The father of capitalism, the economist Adam Smith, argued that what drives business is self-interest. 'It is not from the benevolence of the butcher, the brewer, or the baker that we expect our dinner,' he famously wrote in *The Wealth of Nations*, 'but from their regard to their own interest.'

But to think that that's where Adam Smith's thinking began and ended is to misunderstand his world view. 'No society can surely be flourishing and happy, of which the far greater part of the members are poor and miserable,' he wrote in the same work. Elsewhere he went even further: 'And hence it is, that to feel much for others and little for ourselves, that to restrain our selfish, and to indulge our benevolent affections,' he argued in *The Theory of Moral Sentiments*, 'constitutes the perfection of human nature.' In other words, the father of capitalism recognised that it was about more than profit, growth and wealth. Political economy, to him, had 'two distinct objects: first, to provide a plentiful revenue or subsistence for the people, or, more properly, to enable them to provide such a revenue or subsistence for themselves; and secondly, to supply the state of commonwealth with a revenue sufficient for the public services'. In other words, an ethical dimension to capitalism is not an optional addition – it's an essential aspect of it.

If proof were needed of this basic fact, capitalism's most recent global crisis – the 2008 banking meltdown – provides a textbook example. At bottom, this was not about a failure of a particular economic doctrine or approach but of ethics. In the case of the US sub-prime mortgage scandal bankers acted out of greed, and with no fear of being penalised, to lend money to people who couldn't afford the repayments. Even if you argue that this was a risky rather than a dishonest practice, what happened next was unquestionably unscrupulous, because those bad loans were then securitised and sold on with higher credit ratings than they warranted. The cause of the crash, in other words, was deceit.

Similarly in the UK, investment bankers playing the markets with insanely complicated betting schemes took huge risks with other people's money, without adequately explaining what those risks might be. The whole process was driven by a lack of responsibility, the bankers believing that they were entitled to enormous bonuses when they made money, but not liable to any penalty if their risks did not pay off. In this respect, at least, they were proved right: the UK as a whole paid for the banks' mistakes and had to endure a long period of austerity, while people in the investment banking sector went back to happily receiving massive bonuses and avoiding any criminal penalties.

Once it is accepted that ethics is central to the proper functioning of capitalism – and that a just capitalism will in turn lead to a just society – many other recent developments should be ringing alarm bells. I've been angered to see how some businesses have put their ingenuity and energy into a race to the bottom in terms of employee pay and conditions. Various companies have introduced zero-hours contracts, or have exploited self-employed status by claiming that the people who work for them are not technically their employees, and so do not qualify for sick or holiday pay. Some have been paying their employees at rates well below the minimum wage.

And there are further challenges on the horizon, too. Back in the 1960s, there was a utopian view that greater mechanisation and the increasing use of robots would be a great thing for society – people would be relieved of the burden of boring, repetitive jobs and would be able to enjoy fulfilling leisure time. Now we know that people 'relieved' of their jobs are often condemned to extreme poverty and unemployment. If that increasingly becomes the case, not only will we be wasting lives but we'll be undermining the very prosperity that the automation is supposed to lead to. There's a story that while one of Henry Ford II's managers was showing Walter Reuther, leader of the US automobile workers' union, round a new, highly automated factory in 1953 he asked, 'How are you going to get these robots to pay your union dues?' 'How are you going to get them to buy your cars?' was Reuther's response.

I hope I've adequately explained what I believe capitalism to be. But what precisely do I mean by 'ethical'? At its base, I believe, ethical behaviour is bound by the moral code which society has devised over the centuries, influenced by the world's great religions and shaped by experience, to ensure society's cohesion and long-term future. It's a shared system of beliefs about the ways in which we should interact with each other, based on the principles of honesty, fairness and respect for each other. 'Do as you would be done by' is a good straightforward definition, or, even simpler, Jesus's instruction to 'Love thy neighbour'. Ethical capitalism is about doing our best to ensure that everybody we work with, from staff to customers to the wider community, feels their lives, and their happiness, are improved by what we offer – both materially and emotionally.

When it comes to business, operating ethically does not mean that you have to be a saint and never put a foot wrong. That's impossible, given the mistakes that every business is bound to make. Nor does it involve signing up to one or two 'ethical' buzzwords such as fair trade or going green. And it's not simply about paying your taxes or obeying the letter of the law. For me, it's a whole mindset, which essentially involves three principles:

1. It's all about the people.
   The key to a successful business lies in managing and motivating the workforce so that they give their best to the job. They should be treated honestly and fairly, as should all stakeholders and anyone else that the business comes into contact with: customers, suppliers, contractors (including the cleaners and drivers who tend to get forgotten).

I have found that by treating people well, they appreciate it and will almost always reciprocate and treat my business well.

2. **What goes around comes around.**
    Those who cheat end up being cheated. By the same token, when you give that bit extra, the benefit almost always comes back at some point down the line. I always try to deal with people, not only with honesty and fairness, but with generosity too. In my life I've had so much goodwill and support from people whom I'd been able to help out previously.

3. **You get nowt for nowt.**
    As someone who lives in Yorkshire, I find this expression gets straight to the point. Business essentially comes down to trade, and all trade should be *fair trade*, if it is going to be sustainable. So those business people who think it's clever not to pay their suppliers on time, or who put their ingenuity into devising new ways of giving customers poorer value for money, have got the wrong idea. There might be a short-term advantage in that, but there's long-term failure.

The next chapters will show these principles in action. The first part of the book draws on my direct experience in business, showing what I believe business can and should achieve. I want to demonstrate that, as Adam Smith suggested, an ethical approach to business is not just desirable but necessary.

I believe businesses themselves, their employees and society in general will benefit hugely from ethical capitalism. But it has to be more than an idealistic mission statement, or a PR exercise designed to boost the brand. The ethical approach must be built into the way the business operates every day.

In the second part of the book I look at the wider relationship between business and society. Some private enterprises seek to do the right thing, but what role should the state play in policing those who don't? How do we legislate for keeping capitalism on the straight and narrow – for its own good? And are there areas where private enterprise should not go and which are better left to public bodies?

We need intelligent rules, properly enforced. A game of football without rules would be pointless chaos; the rules have got more sophisticated over time and have made for a better game. I believe we need better rules for business, and harder consequences for those who break them. If we can achieve that, we'll have better capitalism and, with it, a much fairer and happier society.

PART 1

THE ETHICAL BUSINESS

CHAPTER 1

IT'S ALL ABOUT THE PEOPLE

THE EMPLOYEE

'IT'S NOT PERSONAL ... it's strictly business.' Michael Corleone's famous line in *The Godfather* conjures up two very different worlds. There's the world of family and friends, with its bonds of love and loyalty. And there's the completely separate world of business, with its focus on deals and money. As far as Michael is concerned, the two realms never meet.

For those who believe that commercial enterprises exist purely to make money, this is a plausible enough view of the way business should work. At base, it's about generating a profit. How well you behave, how well you treat people in the course of your dealings may or may not be important to you, but they're certainly not central to success. Ultimately, the pursuit of profit has to come first.

Such an ethics-free business approach may seem unattractive to many. But, judged in purely commercial terms, is it effective? Does it create companies that, in purely financial terms, at least, are successful?

A few years back, teams of US business students were invited to take part in a problem-solving competition that involved answering questions via a computer link. If they did well in the first round, they were told, they would be given a competitive advantage in the next. It swiftly became apparent, though, that the competition contained one major design flaw: since scores were not independently validated, team leaders could, if they chose, misreport how their team had done. In other words, they could cheat and get away with it.

In the event, while one group of participants did record their achievement correctly, a second set happily accepted their team leader's decision to nudge their 67 per cent score up to 80 per cent. Their deception went unchallenged.

What neither group knew was that the competition was a set-up by the eminent social psychologist Robert Cialdini. His experiment was not, however, designed to establish whether people cheat if given the chance – we know from bitter experience that some will. Instead, he was interested in finding out what effect cheating has on people's subsequent behaviour. The next round, therefore, was the real test. Here Professor Cialdini arranged for each member of each group to be given a business case history and asked to answer a series of questions about it without consulting their teammates. Intriguingly, this time, those who had falsely claimed to do well in the first round uniformly performed worse than those who had been honest. The true scores from the previous round had suggested that they were all pretty evenly matched. Now those from the cheating team scored, on average, 20 per cent lower than their honest opponents. Cialdini studied their answers and came to the conclusion that the reason for this was that they tended to give up when the questions got tough. It was, he said, as though they lacked the 'energy or motivation to continue'.

Professor Cialdini's explanation for this apparently surprising behaviour seems to me to be an entirely convincing one. Although we will all misbehave from time to time, although we may well occasionally cheat or lie, most of us have a sense of right and wrong. We live in societies that have established certain social conventions over the centuries, maybe based on religious principles, maybe derived from the practical experience of what it takes for communities to live well together. We know it's in our long-term interests to be honest with others, to help them when we can, to avoid doing things that might cause them harm – that is, if we wish to be treated the same way. So when we're encouraged to depart from these norms, a tension arises between what we fundamentally believe to be right and what we're being invited to do, and this tension undermines us.

A working environment that seems unprincipled or dishonest, then, can sap our energies. There's also overwhelming evidence to suggest that it increases levels of individual stress. But what Professor Cialdini found that is perhaps most striking is that a business that encourages sharp practice among its employees is itself highly likely to be defrauded by them. As he puts it: 'those who cheat for you will cheat against you'. If people find themselves working in an organisation that has no moral compass, and that is geared to chasing sales at any cost, extracting the maximum out of the customer and circumventing statutory regulations, their behaviour will come to reflect that culture. After all, if your employer is happy to ride roughshod over people all the time, why would you choose to act any differently? Your own behaviour will start to mimic that of the organisation you serve – and not to that organisation's advantage.

The recent scandal at the US bank Wells Fargo offers a textbook example of the toxic effects of a bad business culture. According to the UK Fraud Advisory Panel, regulators found that between 2011 and 2016 bank employees created hundreds of thousands of fraudulent accounts on behalf of clients without their consent and without letting on to their managers what they were up to. As the panel's report, *Businesses Behaving Badly*, puts it: 'Wells Fargo's CEO claimed that the 5,300 employees accused of opening 1.5m false bank accounts and 465,000 fraudulent credit cards had all acted without management's knowledge.' But the fact that the managers didn't know doesn't mean that they weren't in some way responsible. In the words of the report, 'red flags were all over the bank's culture'. Staff had been subjected to 'performance-based pay, intense sales pressure, frequent bullying, and threats of sacking'. It was scarcely surprising, then, that some should have gone rogue.

The world of banking has been littered with similar examples in recent years. In a court case in 2017, for example, it emerged that six financiers, including a former senior HBOS manager, had been guilty of operating a scam that involved £245 million worth of fraudulent loans. The corporate banking manager at HBOS's Reading branch had made huge loans to small business customers, knowing full well they would not be able to repay. When they had inevitably defaulted, he had then referred them to his associates' 'turnaround' consultancy, which proceeded to rip them off and in many cases reduce them to bankruptcy.

Managers at the bank may have been unaware that anything was wrong, but it's clear that, as at

Wells Fargo, a culture existed that allowed or encouraged bad behaviour. Controls were lax: HBOS's computer system permitted credit to be given to clients without investigation or approval by senior management. There was an emphasis on quick results. And it was very likely that the fact that bonuses were linked to short-term profitability was a disincentive to senior executives' questioning what was really going on at the Reading branch. It's certainly a fact that the fraudulent loans generated arrangement fees and loan volumes that made this particular enterprise look profitable and generated bonuses for many.

The testimony of Kweku Adoboli, a former trader at UBS in London, points out very clearly the link between a company's culture and the behaviour of individual members of staff. Adoboli's name hit the headlines in 2011 when he admitted responsibility for a series of disastrous trades that led to a £1.4 billion loss. He was convicted of fraud and sentenced to seven years in prison. After his release he sought to explain what had happened in these terms: 'Good people can do bad things when we take away their moral anchors and supports. Any of us can find ourselves in that situation.' And he went on to argue that 'Complex, high-pressure, highly-conflicted working environments leave individuals unable to make morally-sound decisions.'

Some might argue that banks are exceptional in this regard (though, in fairness, it would be wrong to tar all banks with the same brush). They are high-pressure environments where vast sums of money are at stake. For historical reasons they have evolved a system of bonuses and incentives which have had the effect of putting staff first and customers very much second. And because they are so central to the global economy, they tend to get bailed out when things go wrong rather than be punished for bad behaviour. To that extent, they are in a win-win position.

But all the evidence suggests that a bad culture leads to bad behaviour regardless of the business sector in which it is to be found. Individual members of staff in a poorly run manufacturer or retailer may not be in a position to perpetrate frauds at the level achieved by some bankers, but they will still find less headline-grabbing ways of stealing from their employer. Some £40 million-worth of staff fraud carried out in UK businesses was reported to police in 2016. One has to assume that much more went undetected. In the retail sector it's estimated that employee pilfering from stores and warehouses – or 'shrinkage' as it is euphemistically called – accounts for 1 per cent to 2 per cent of turnover each year – a vast sum overall.

Worryingly, those people guilty of fraud and theft often include highly experienced staff, according to accountancy firm PricewaterhouseCoopers (PwC), which produces an annual report on economic crime. It explains this phenomenon in the following terms in its 2016 report: 'the older we get, the more willing we are to break the rules and to act according to our own personal moral compass.' That may well be true. But, of course, it's precisely these older, more senior staff who set the company culture. Their decision to behave in this way creates the environment for fraud elsewhere.

The fact that fraud and theft so often go unreported says a lot about the companies in which they take place. People generally have an inkling if something untoward is going on within an organisation. If they don't do something about it, that suggests that they may think that it's generally accepted practice ('senior colleagues always fiddle their expenses'). Or they may feel they don't owe sufficient loyalty to the company to act. They may worry that they won't be listened to. Or they may fear that they will be punished or bullied for whistle-blowing, particularly if the guilty party is senior to them. Grim media stories about the terrible injustices whistle-blowers have suffered suggest that one sure indicator of a bad organisation is the way it treats people who have raised legitimate concerns.

* *

Fraud and theft are hallmarks of a poor company culture, but they're not the only ones. Staff turnover and absenteeism are also crucial indicators. Some staff churn is inevitable, as people move away or are offered a better or preferable job elsewhere. But high levels of staff turnover are always a sign that something is fundamentally wrong. It may be that the pay is too low or the level of stress too high. There may be aggression and mistrust in the workplace, or bad relations with third parties.

If a significant number of staff are regularly absent, it's also a sure indication of a deep underlying problem. Stress is the UK's second biggest cause of short-term absences from work (minor illnesses make up the largest category). And all too often it is work related. People find themselves struggling with too heavy a workload. Or they face bullying by colleagues or managers. Or they have to cope with poor or ineffectual management. It should come as no surprise that one of Professor Cialdini's findings in the US was that employees of companies which were not highly rated for their ethical standards tended to feel more stressed and were more likely to quit than those who worked for companies that enjoyed a good reputation.

There's a human cost here, of course. But as with fraud and theft there's a cost for the companies involved, too. Businesses may think that high staff turnover is not a problem, as long as there is a ready supply of new applicants. But in reality, a constantly changing workforce is a big drag on productivity. Moreover it eats into profits. A 2014 report by Oxford Economics put the cost of replacing a staff member at £30,000. This may seem implausibly high, but it's worth bearing in mind not only the expense of hiring and training a new recruit, but the inefficiencies involved in the three to seven months that that person takes to bed in to their new job and reach 'optimum productivity level'.

Absenteeism is astonishingly expensive, too. It's been estimated that UK rates stand at over 2 per cent in the private sector and 3.5 per cent in the public sector. According to The Chartered Institute of Personnel and Development (CIPD) which runs an annual survey of absence management, that translates into 6.3 days per employee per year. Given that some will only ever take two or three days off sick a year, it's clear that others take many more. One way and another, the cost to employers is reckoned to be in the region of £16 billion a year.

Given the link between absence and stress, I think it's telling that, according to the CIPD reports, only a third of employers monitor the cost of sickness absence. It suggests to me that there are a significant number of companies out there who are not that concerned with the welfare of their staff. If they were, they would be examining very closely the reasons why so many of their colleagues need to take time away from work. The fact that they're not suggests a culture that allowed the absenteeism problem to arise in the first place. Of course, companies who are aware of the problem need to act very carefully, and make sure they are tackling underlying causes, not the outcomes. Amazon was rightly criticised when it was found that its policy for warehouse staff, who were threatened with the sack if they clocked up too many 'points' for being off sick, penalised people who were genuinely ill. Ironically, of course, this policy will have added to the stress of those workers affected. Penalising absenteeism or, conversely, rewarding attendance can lead to sick people dragging themselves into work when they should really be at home, instead of infecting everyone. It's a wholly immoral practice, in my view.

So there's a paradox here. All the evidence suggests that if employees are badly treated, the company as a whole will suffer: it will attract poor-quality, often unmotivated employees, who may well defraud it or take extended leaves of absence, and who will quit as soon as they can. Yet some companies are prepared to risk all this for short-term gain and profit, not recognising that in the process they are racking up costs and running the risk of forfeiting future success.

Forget for a moment that poor treatment of staff is morally wrong. Even for businesses narrowly focused on making a quick buck, it makes no financial sense.

By the same token, organisations that create a culture based on fairness, honesty and respect reap the rewards. They acquire motivated, hard-working staff who are there for the long haul. It's no coincidence that many of the world's most successful companies are those that are also rated as the best to work for (which is, essentially, the message of *In Search of Excellence*).

That point perhaps needs to be emphasised. All too often when the word 'ethical' is bandied about in a business context, the image conjured up in people's minds is of a company that is trying to save the rainforest, or cut back on global warming, or use sustainable raw materials, or give some of its proceeds to charity. These are all thoroughly praiseworthy activities. But to my mind they count for little if that company is exploiting its own staff. They become no more than a smokescreen and a bid for good publicity. Ethical businesses are ethical employers.

So when I say that I think a company such as Riverford Organics is an ethical company, I'm only partly thinking of the nature of the business sector in which they sit. For those unfamiliar with it, it's a company that started pretty much with the founder, Guy Watson, delivering his organic produce to friends in Devon by wheelbarrow, and has since developed into a network of five farms and delivery franchises that send out 47,000 veg boxes weekly across the UK. It does all the things that you would expect such a company to do: it has a strong commitment to protecting the environment, safeguarding animal welfare and tackling food waste; it runs community and educational events; it supports a charity in Africa.

But what is most striking is that it treats its own people well, offering secure jobs and pensions in a sector traditionally characterised by insecure employment and very low pay. Watson has spoken out against the exploitation of workers, particularly migrant workers, in British agriculture, arguing: 'Cheap food has too often come at the cost of a return to Victorian working practices.' His ultimate ambition is that the company should be employee owned, since he strongly believes that in that way 'our staff will be more fulfilled and engaged, we will learn faster, be more innovative and, ultimately, better at what we do.'

It's perhaps worth adding that Riverford Organics generates a turnover of £50 million and that it is continuing to grow. And it is proving profitable in a notoriously precarious industry where many farms struggle to survive or are heavily dependent on EU subsidies.

* *

I'm very aware that phrases like 'treating people well' and 'creating a culture based on fairness, honesty and respect' can sound frustratingly vague. They also smack of that insincere tagline so many businesses like to use: 'Our people are our greatest asset.' So what do they really mean in practice, and how does one go about instilling them into an organisation?

One key point needs to be stated at the outset: while treating all employees at all times with honesty and fairness may sound the obvious thing to do, it is also far from simple to achieve. One of the commonest criticisms levelled at even the best-intentioned companies is that they can all too easily become guilty of double standards. They may have put together an impressive code of conduct, or held staff forums where they talk about corporate values, but then there's the moment when they fail to live up to their own standards and they end up looking like hypocrites. Creating an ethically minded company is not something that's achieved the moment a list of company values has been put together. It's a process that involves very hard work and requires constant attention.

It also has to permeate every action that a company takes, which is why for me this process of creating an ethical company begins right at the very beginning of the job cycle – with the recruitment ad – and not only continues through recruitment, the setting of pay and conditions, ongoing staff welfare, and so on, but also requires regular maintenance and improvement. If one link of this complex chain is weak, or is allowed to become weak, ultimately the chain will break.

Take the apparently simple task of putting together a job ad. It ought to go without saying that this should be an honest description of what the role on offer involves. Yet I've noticed that companies are often tempted to exaggerate or even misrepresent the scope or nature of a post in the belief that this will secure the best candidate. The fact is, though, that even this very minor departure from the truth will almost invariably backfire, because it will attract people who are either unsuited for the role or who will become disillusioned when they discover that it's not all that it's cracked up to be. Many years ago when I was advising the supermarket chain Asda I found myself rather taken aback to discover that their recruitment ads featured great-looking athletic people climbing mountains, even though the actual job involved sitting at a checkout. It seemed to me, at the very least, a misleading way to attract new members of staff, and I wasn't at all surprised to learn that it hadn't delivered the desired results. It confirmed in my own mind the basic rule that if you want the right people for the job, you at least have to describe it accurately.

Once candidates have been lined up for interview, it's absolutely essential to make sure, not just that they're qualified to do the job on offer, but that they understand and take on board the company's wider values. That doesn't mean they have to be absolute paragons of virtue. Sadly, such individuals are few and far between. But it's dangerous to take on someone only because they tick particular aptitude boxes.

The Richer Sounds approach to recruitment may seem over the top to some, but it exemplifies what I mean by this. If we were simply box-ticking, the logical thing for us to do as retailers would be to seek out red-hot salespeople. But we don't. The most important quality we look for in a recruit is friendliness: we need staff who can not only talk to customers, but who can listen to what they say. Passion and enthusiasm are important, too. We like applicants who are enthusiastic about the products we sell, about dealing with customers, and about life in general. Overall, our policy is to hire for personality and train for skills, and I think that basic rule should hold for most organisations, though obviously the level and nature of skills required will vary from company to company.

Most companies offer a job to a particular candidate after one or two interviews. We don't. Instead, we invite people who seem promising at first interview to spend at least one 'trial day' (for which they are paid) working at one of our stores. This obviously enables the candidate to find out whether he or she is suited to the demands of retail work. At the same time, it allows the store manager to judge whether the applicant would make a good member of the team. Are they helpful and courteous with customers? Are they keen to work and pull their weight? Do they demonstrate common sense and the ability to learn? The other members of the store team also give their opinion on how they thought the candidate performed. No one is ever hired without having had a trial day.

We believe this is the right approach to recruitment, one that embodies those key principles of honesty and fairness. The candidate gains an honest experience of the job and has a good chance to show us who they are and what they can do, while we are able to take the time to appraise them properly and fairly.

A candidate who does well during their trial period goes forward to an interview with our human resources department and ultimately with our Operations Director. If he or she is approved centrally, references and background checks are followed up carefully: we want to be as confident as possible that the person is honest.

I realise this may sound like a lot of fuss for an entry-level sales post, but there are two compelling reasons for our approach here. First, we need to be confident that everyone we employ is a good fit (anyone who has ever worked in a business will know what a corrosive effect even one unsuitable member of staff can have). Second, we want to recruit for the long term. We want people who want to be with us. We seek people who are career orientated and who are keen to work their way up. Indeed we do our damnedest to recruit from within. It's no coincidence that seven out of nine of our directors started out working in the shops (the exceptions being the marketing and finance director posts, for which particular specialist skills were required). That way we keep the people who understand the business best. That way, too, we demonstrate to colleagues who are committed to us that we reciprocate their loyalty. It would be wholly wrong and demotivating to cut off their promotion prospects by bringing in others over their heads unless we had to.

This central pillar of fairness extends to pay as well. A company can win any number of prizes for its charity work and display any number of certificates for social projects it may have supported, but in my view these achievements count for nothing if it is not also paying at the very least a living wage. (By living wage, I mean the one set by the Living Wage

Foundation, which is based on the real cost of living and does not discriminate against young people; I'm not referring to the inadequate government national living wage, which, in addition, discriminates against young people).

We seem to have become a society where wages are seen as unnecessary for some. Graduates are expected to find a job by undertaking lengthy unpaid internships. Some local authorities are trying to deal with reduced budgets by getting 'volunteers' to run libraries and other community facilities – the volunteers sometimes being the redundant former employees. Qualified care workers, making home visits to elderly clients, find that their agency will only pay for the fifteen minutes they spend with each client, not the twenty minutes it takes them to drive to the next visit. This idea that it's OK not to pay people for their time, or to pay as little as you can get away with, has pervaded the economy. But fair pay for a job well done should be an essential element of the contract we all enter into when we join the world of work. Obviously, what precisely constitutes 'fair' in this context is open to debate, but at the very least the money on offer has to reflect what the phrase 'Living Wage' implies.

If a fair approach to wages is essential, then fairness has to extend to all other aspects of a job that involve some form of remuneration. People take on work for many reasons, not all to do with money. They may enjoy the companionship that employment offers. They may find the challenges that a job throws up to be stimulating. They may discover that it fulfils their creative or intellectual interests. These are powerful drivers. But the moment perceived unfairness sneaks in, those drivers collapse. Research in the US has shown over and over again that poorly designed or unequal incentives can have a devastating effect on people's morale and performance. If you receive an unexpected bonus of £10,000, you will probably be delighted. But if you then find out that a colleague doing precisely the same job has received £15,000, you won't focus on the money you were given but on the additional £5,000 your colleague gained. Far from being pleased, you will feel outraged.

This is precisely why promotions – which, of course, involve a salary increase – and bonuses – in those organisations where they are paid – have to be so carefully handled. The moment that a promotion is given for any other reason than outstanding performance, the effect on others can be debilitating. And the criteria for outstanding performance need to be clear, too. In retail it is clear that a good sales assistant is one who achieves a high number of profitable sales. But raw sales figures alone will not necessarily give an accurate picture of an individual's performance. The store's overall performance may suffer if sales are high, but goods are returned as being unsuitable, or if customers are so annoyed, having been pressured into buying, that they never shop there again. Outstanding performance in this sector, then, means not only achieving sales but giving excellent customer service and meeting customers' needs. Only when these vital elements are taken into consideration is a sales person's true worth and potential apparent.

The same rules apply to bonuses and other financial incentives. At Richer Sounds we have a clear bonus payment mechanism in place. Sales assistants receive a commission on most items they sell. They are also rewarded if a customer rates the quality of overall service as 'excellent' on the questionnaires we hand out (for the very occasional 'poor' there is a financial penalty, though it's not deducted from basic salary). And to make sure that it's not just those on the shop floor who benefit from success, we give all our central departments a profit share at the end of the financial year. I'm not a believer in flat pay or flat organisational structures – I believe that these can be demotivating. But I do believe that remuneration and career advancement have to be treated equitably, and to be seen to be equitable. (Incidentally, we have a rule at Richer Sounds that any proposed changes to employee pay and conditions have to be ratified by our Colleague Council.)

It's also important to provide the wherewithal to enable people to progress. A training programme is therefore key – not only because it will enhance an employee's skills and make them more valuable to the company, but because it demonstrates the company's ongoing commitment to the employee. Too many organisations, in my view, provide training only at the outset and so give out – no doubt, inadvertently – the message that they're not that interested in an employee's long-term future. Our approach at Richer Sounds is to devote every weekday morning to staff training (hence the reason why our stores don't open to customers until midday between Monday and Friday). It helps the business because colleagues are able to acquire knowledge of new products and so pass on informed advice to customers. But it also shows colleagues that we don't want them to stand still. Colleagues in other areas of the business also receive regular training.

To achieve all this, constant monitoring is required. It's not uncommon to find a business setting a general direction and then leaving people to get on with it. In my own company we measure and assess obsessively. We monitor every aspect of the business via what we call the Richer Sounds Dashboard – a report set out rather like the dashboard of a car, that gives the managers and directors who are 'driving' the business the information they need about what is happening at any one time, so that problems are signalled early on and dealt with swiftly (for example, an unusual drop in sales figures can be seen within days, rather than the directors having to wait for quarterly reports). At the same time, we constantly monitor individual performance. Every colleague has a score card. Into this are fed their results from training and tests, their sales figures, and customer service feedback obtained from the questionnaires which customers fill in about the service they received from the named sales assistant. Everyone can therefore see how they are doing: there is no secrecy, discrimination or favouritism. The score card offers another advantage too: quite simply, our colleagues thrive on it. They tend to be competitive people and they want to get noticed and to get on. Key to this process is colleagues understanding how and why they are being measured, and being able to speak up if they're not happy with the way that the process is being managed.

Companies in other sectors will obviously need to measure other outcomes. A manufacturing company, say, will focus on quality of output rather than customer service. For an airline, safety will be a fundamental consideration. Logistics companies will concentrate on ensuring that their employees are making deliveries in the right place, at the right time, in good condition. But whatever the business's primary goal, it must recruit, train, motivate and reward its staff to deliver that. And it has to judge its own performance, too.

Just as sharp practice in business is self-defeating, so a drive to operate fairly is more than its own reward. It makes financial sense, too. To focus briefly on my own company again for a moment. I mentioned earlier that theft and fraud are a significant problem for UK businesses, accounting for between 1 and 2 per cent of turnover each year. At Richer Sounds, shrinkage is barely 0.1 per cent, saving us several million pounds a year compared with the average. Absenteeism in the UK, as I've said, ranges between 2 per cent in the private sector and 3.5 per cent in the public sector. At Richer Sounds the figure is at the lower end. Our staff turnover is lower than the norm, too, and when you bear in mind that it typically costs us thousands of pounds to recruit and train a new staff member, the savings that good levels of retention give us are considerable. Moreover, experienced employees tend to be more efficient and productive; and they enhance the company's reputation with its customers, who feel reassured when they're being served by people who clearly know what they're doing. That's the reason why we state length of service alongside the photographs of the staff who appear in our ads (and we don't use models).

But it goes beyond that. Disaffected staff offer bad service, and bad service drives away customers. It's been estimated that every unhappy customer will tell up to twenty other people about their experience (though only one customer in twenty bothers to complain direct to the service provider). Contented staff, by contrast, encourage repeat business. What's more, I've invariably found that when people are treated well, the tendency is for them to reciprocate – by working hard, and by contributing their enthusiasm and ideas. They feel motivated, morale rises, and productivity and profitability improve as a result.

The sector in which I operate – electronics retail – is a highly competitive one. We face competition from all quarters, on the high street, in retail parks and on the internet. Any one of them may suddenly decide to undercut us in a bid to draw our customers away. The fact that we're still in business and still profitable over forty years after I established that first branch of Richer Sounds at London Bridge suggests that, even if we don't get everything right, our focus on treating our staff fairly has given us staying power. To that extent virtue has proved not only its own reward, but has come with a financial reward, too.

CHAPTER 2

WHAT GOES AROUND COMES AROUND

THE CUSTOMER

IT'S HARD TO imagine a world without pizza. Over 40 per cent of the population of the US eat it at least once a week, and, according to one survey, it's the most popular choice in UK restaurants. It's fair to say, then, that a business dedicated to takeaway pizza has a captive market, and it's therefore not too surprising that a takeaway pizza company such as Domino's should have been so successful. Founded in 1960, it grew steadily through the next decades, and by 2006 had not only opened its 5,000th US store but was turning over $1.4 billion globally. Its business formula was a simple one: cheap food delivered quickly.

And then things began to go wrong. Cheap started to mean poor quality – 'Domino's pizza crust is like cardboard,' said one customer; 'Microwave pizza is far superior,' said another. Customer service declined. The low point was reached in 2008 when a video apparently showing two Domino's employees messing around with and contaminating pizzas before they were sent out was posted on YouTube. The video may well have been a stunt, but a million people saw it. By 2009 the company's revenues were falling.

It was at this point that a new CEO, Patrick Doyle, was appointed, and he immediately set out to try to turn things round. His recovery plan involved a number of initiatives. First, he got the company to improve their ingredients and recipes, submitting them to blind taste tests, and ultimately bringing them to the point where they were coming out ahead of their direct rivals, Papa John's and Pizza Hut. Then he revamped Domino's ordering process, installing a highly versatile, user-friendly system. Now you could order by texting Domino's the pizza-slice emoji. There was a new, easy-to-use app that placed an order automatically after ten seconds. You could even follow the progress of your pizza through preparation, cooking and delivery via Domino's Pizza Tracker.

The ultimate bold move was a US advertising campaign that addressed customers' complaints head on – and apologised. Domino's executives appeared on screen, acknowledging customer comments like 'Worst excuse for pizza I ever had' and accepting the criticism. Patrick Doyle was quoted as saying, 'We think that going out there and being this honest really breaks through to people in a way that most advertising does not.'

The company's subsequent turnaround has been remarkable. The mea culpa ads may have been a risky strategy: people could very easily only have heard the complaints and not taken on board Domino's follow-up message that 'We've changed'. But because change really was taking place, customers started to flock back. Domino's have recently enjoyed eight consecutive quarters of double-digit sales growth. Since 2010, their share price has increased 1,200 per cent.

To my mind the Domino's turnaround story perfectly demonstrates three of the most important elements that determine whether or not a company appeals to its prospective customers: quality of product, quality of service, openness of culture. At the same time, they also show just how interdependent these elements are. Domino's apology ads were a master-stroke, but such openness would have been a disaster if the company had not actually improved its pizzas. If it had improved them but failed to tackle the issues it clearly had with service, the turnaround would not have succeeded.

And recovery also relied heavily on transforming the relationship the company had with its staff. A business is like a very delicate ecosystem. Every component part of it counts and every part has an impact on everything else. People often ask me whether ultimately it's the employee or the customer who is more important to commercial success. To my mind it's not a valid question. In the business ecosystem each element has a vital role and each element is connected to all the others. That's why creating the right overarching culture is so crucial. Without it, things fall apart.

That's also why precisely the same considerations that apply to the internal workings of a business apply to its relationship with its customers. You can't have a company that will be successful in the long term if you pay your staff well but cheat your customers, or if you offer a great product but treat your staff badly. I think it's telling in this respect that companies regularly rated by *Which?* magazine as the best retailers, in terms of customer service, tend to be the ones that are also reckoned to be good employers: John Lewis, Lush, Lakeland, Apple, Toolstation, Waterstones and Screwfix, among them. Richer Sounds, I'm proud to say, has been consistently in the top five over the last decade. It's also telling that the same names crop up year after year in the bottom ten.

Perhaps the piece of the business jigsaw puzzle that best demonstrates this interconnectedness of all parts of a business is price. All of us like a bargain. It therefore certainly seems entirely plausible that if something is cheap enough, other considerations won't apply. And it certainly is possible to build a business purely on price, particularly now that the internet makes it so easy for 'plunder hunters', as retailers nickname them, to shop around.

The problem is that this approach makes for an unstable customer base. If customers don't like or trust the business, they will hotfoot it to a competitor, on the high street or on the web, as soon as someone else offers a lower price. If cheapness comes at the price of good service, they may buy one item but be dubious about repeating the experience. Either way, it then becomes necessary for the bargain basement company to spend a lot of money on marketing and promotions to attract new customers. In my view, that's not a good way to build a profitable company.

Ratner's the jewellers offers the classic example of the perils of a focus only on price. During the course of the 1980s they became a familiar sight on the nation's high streets, offering cut-price bargains and cheap ranges. In 1991, however, boss Gerald Ratner made an unguarded speech to the Institute of Directors in which he let slip the remark, 'We also do cut-glass sherry decanters complete with six glasses on a silver-plated tray that your butler can serve you drinks on, for £4.95. People say "How can you sell this for such a low price?" I say, "Because it's total crap."' He then added that his stores' earrings were 'cheaper than an M&S prawn sandwich but probably wouldn't last as long.' When the speech was made public, consumers turned on him in fury. Almost overnight £500 million was wiped from the value of the company. Customers had never been under any illusion that Ratner's products were anything but cheap and cheerful. But that note of offhand disrespect for consumers was enough to tip the scales.

Really successful businesses at the budget end of the market may concentrate relentlessly on price, but they also know that in today's ever more competitive world, that's not enough. Supermarkets are a case in point. Food retail is one of the most fought over sectors of the consumer market, with at least ten major players in the UK market. Competition has driven down prices to the point where the average family's expenditure on food today is only a third of what it was fifty or so years ago as a percentage of their income, and profit margins are correspondingly incredibly thin – typically in the low single digits. Yet even at the budget end, the relatively new players Aldi and Lidl focus relentlessly on both good quality food and good customer service: they want people to be happy with what is on offer and how they are treated (Aldi was named the Institute of Customer Service best supermarket for customer satisfaction in 2017; they also treat their staff very well).

One would like to think that they do this because it's the right thing to do. But as I have already intimated, there are compelling commercial reasons, too. In the first place, great service is an important differentiating factor. Any business operating in a competitive market has to distinguish itself from its rivals and convince customers it is better. The products might be broadly the same in a number of places; what varies is how the products are sold, and also what the after-sales service is like. Bottom-end bargain chains tend to be indistinguishable from one another and so rarely acquire customer loyalty. When a vigorous new entrant comes into the market they don't have the goodwill resources to survive, and so end up going to the wall.

Secondly, great service prompts impulse buying. We've all had the experience of going into a shop as something has caught our eye, seething with frustration because the sales staff are nowhere in sight or are studiously ignoring us, and ultimately walking out in annoyance, empty-handed. Conversely, the right approach from a sales assistant – friendly but not pushy – can be the factor that tips us over into a decision to buy.

Finally, great service brings customers back. People can be attracted into buying a product or service with special offers and deals (at Richer Sounds we certainly specialise in deals). But price advantages can only ever be short-term, so the way in which they are treated becomes the conversion tool that turns new customers into long-term customers. Indeed, there is no point in having a promotion *unless* it can be backed up by excellent service. A reliance on price alone simply means that people graze from one bargain outlet to another. After all, it is so easy now to shop around on the internet in search of cheap buys that businesses have to offer much more than low prices if they want repeat customers.

It's also worth bearing in mind the obvious but often forgotten truth that repeat customers are the most profitable. You don't have to advertise to reach them or spend marketing resources on reaching out to potential new customers to replace them or put together expensive introductory offers or promotions. According to a US study carried out by SumAll in 2013, somewhere between 25 per cent and 40 per cent of the total revenues of the most stable businesses they examined came from returning customers. These customers were also most likely to be the ones who helped sustain the companies they supported in difficult economic times: 'businesses with 40%

repeat customers generated nearly 50% more revenue than similar businesses with only 10% repeat customers,' the study suggested.

It therefore seems totally bizarre to me that some companies would think it clever practice to go out of their way to alienate existing customers. Why would an insurance company offer cover at a special price to attract a new customer and yet increase premiums for the same package to an existing one? Why would a bank or a phone company offer preferential rates only to the people they don't already serve? It's baffling. I know they're relying on customer inertia, but I suspect that as people become more savvy and it becomes ever easier to find out what rival deals there are out there, customers will defect from such concerns in steadily increasing numbers. It's a cynical and foolish approach that deserves to backfire.

The fact is that a well-served and loyal customer base makes for a thriving business. Richer Sounds now has more than a million people in its VIP Club, where they can secure better prices on some products, longer warranties, and product demonstrations outside normal store opening hours. They benefit from their loyalty to us, just as we benefit from our loyalty to them. They also serve as our ambassadors, recommending us to other potential customers who, research shows, are far more likely to be persuaded by an enthusiastic thumbs up from a friend than by a slick, expensive advertisement.

Of course, some businesses operate in complex sectors – often ones with very high barriers to entry – where the lack of competition that helps keeps other companies honest doesn't apply, or, at least, doesn't apply to the same extent. Budget airlines are a case in point: the expense of acquiring and running aircraft, the complexities of negotiating airport slots and facilities, and the infrastructure required to run services are sufficient to deter most potential new entrants. And this perhaps helps to explain why budget airlines are among those businesses that don't generally receive the best press. Their websites can be very difficult to negotiate. The price you think you are paying at the beginning of a transaction has a tendency not to resemble the one you are finally faced with. In the short term they can get away with this – the still cheap prices they offer are too strong an incentive. But it's not the best way to build passenger loyalty, and the danger with that is that as and when a new player does appear, your passengers will desert you.

This is particularly the case now that we live in a world where feedback is so constant and so public. For a well-run business, feedback is essential. It gives you an insight into your customers and what they want. It also serves as an early warning system, alerting you to problems in good time, and so enabling you to take action before they spiral out of control. At Richer Sounds, we include a short feedback card with every receipt (the incentive to fill it in being entry into a monthly prize draw) which asks a few questions about the customer and their buying habits, why they decided to come to us, and whether they were happy with the way they were treated and what they bought. The 25,000 or so that are completed each year, and which are then studied at our quarterly director-level Customer Service Group meetings, help us trouble-shoot, plan and refine. They also provide us with an invaluable window into the future, since they often give the first indication that customers' tastes might be changing and that they might be looking for something new or different.

Additional feedback comes from our Facebook and Twitter sites, from numerous web forums and Google reviews and from the 'We're Listening' cards we leave on the counter, which can be filled in by anyone who visits one of our shops (in that way if someone receives poor service and decides not to purchase from us, they can still use the card to make us aware of the problem). All these allow us to engage directly with people: we monitor key feedback on a daily basis, responding to any critical comments as quickly as possible. If there's a complaint, I deal with it personally.

But feedback is a two-edged sword, and companies that fall foul of it can be hugely – sometimes irretrievably – damaged by it. Research by BrightLocal, a search engine optimisation company, suggests that these days most people looking to place work with a local business will check online reviews first, and that nearly half of those won't go ahead and choose a business if it hasn't received at the very least a four-star rating. Media stories constantly emerge of hotels and restaurants driven to the brink by a rash of bad customer reviews. Not all reviews are fair, but the cumulative effect of hostile reviews can be devastating. It might be possible to reject a single bad one as sour grapes from a difficult customer. Multiple negative reviews suggest that the wisdom of crowds is at work. And bad reviews can be triggered by any aspect of a company or the service it offers that its customers deem not to have come up to scratch.

Take the story of Mast Brothers, a US artisanal chocolate company. Back in 2006 Rick and Michael Mast were making chocolate from scratch in a Brooklyn apartment and selling it at local flea markets. Within a few years they were offering twelve varieties of chocolate bar, and selling them at $10 a time. But their claims that the chocolate was made from scratch came into question in 2015 when a food blogger suggested that, in the early years at least, the brothers had melted down chocolate from a high-end supplier and then added their own ingredients, and that they had not always therefore been the 'bean to bar' operation they held themselves to be. The fact that the scandal emerged years after the company had switched to a genuine bean-to-bar process didn't stop adverse coverage and a significant drop in sales that Christmas. Nor did the fact that the actual quality and taste of the chocolate was never in question stem the criticism.

Which makes one wonder what the long-term cost to Volkswagen will be for the 2015 emissions scandal, in the aftermath of which the company was forced to admit in the US that they had modified the software in certain diesel models so as to falsify the level of polluting emissions. The immediate consequences were the withdrawal of affected models from sales and price reductions on other products to win over dubious consumers. Billions of dollars had to be set aside to resolve the crisis. The cost to Volkswagen's reputation is harder to measure.

All this suggests that 'the market' is self-correcting: terrible customer service, poor or misleading products, bad value for money will all be found out and punished. Good companies survive. Unethical companies go to the wall.

But, of course, it's not quite that simple, at least in the short term.

Because businesses are such complex mechanisms, even the smallest of fault lines can widen into problems that can prove slow and difficult to eradicate. Incentives and bonuses demonstrate the dangers. Properly organised they are a fair reward for good service. But when they are treated simply as sales or performance bonuses, the rot very quickly sets in. Every transaction should be a reciprocal arrangement that benefits both the seller and the purchaser. In a retail or service environment that might well mean that the customer ends up leaving the shop or office empty-handed because in the course of their conversation with a member of the sales team it becomes apparent to both parties that what is on offer is not suitable in their case.

This is certainly the approach we've adopted at Richer Sounds. I want our customers to understand the details of what is on offer ('take a look at these two TVs: the picture refresh rate on this one is 20 per cent better than that one, so is better for sports, but it's £50 more'), and then only to buy what meets their particular requirements. (This is the reason why we never talk about a particular product being 'good' or 'bad' − the last time I discovered that one of our sales people had described an item a customer was keen on as 'bad', we ended up contacting the customer, giving her the product free, and taking flowers round to her house.) If a customer can't find what they want in one of our shops, or aren't completely sure about the suitability of what is on offer, I don't want to make a sale. Our trading philosophy as well as our incentive scheme is based on that principle. I always say to our sales colleagues that achieving an immediate profit by persuading a customer to buy something that isn't right for them is both wrong and crazy. We should be aiming to keep a customer for life, not for one transaction.

But when incentives are badly constructed, the outcomes will be bad, too. It's an area of human behaviour that has received a lot of scholarly attention in recent years, but perhaps just one example will serve to demonstrate what I mean. In their book *The Why Axis*, behavioural economists John List and Uri Gneezy describe how a day-care centre in Tel Aviv tried to tackle the problem of parents turning up late to pick up their children by imposing a small fine. The tactic, however, backfired. Parents came to the conclusion that this policy meant that it was all right to pick up their children late provided they paid for the privilege, and the number of latecomers actually went up. The incentive had sent out the wrong signals. The effect was precisely the opposite to the one that was intended.

In the same way, staff incentives based on very narrow, badly thought-through criteria almost invariably result in bad behaviour. The retail sector offers plenty of depressing examples. The problem is even more apparent in the financial and services sectors where the products on offer are often highly complex and the customer is therefore much more easily misled. The banking bonus culture in the first decade of the century, for example, encouraged individual bankers to make foolish loan decisions, to construct unstable and complicated products, and to provide credit cards to customers who they were fully aware were not in a position to pay the money back. The mis-selling of payment protection insurance (PPI) was similarly propelled by a bonus culture that rewarded the selling of expensive insurance packages to people who often didn't need them and in some cases weren't even aware that they had bought them. Rewarding people simply for carrying out a transaction, regardless of the wisdom of that transaction, is a recipe for disaster.

But for most organisations the biggest obstacle to the fair and ethical treatment of customers is that seemingly most simple of concepts: the truth. Telling the truth demands that you have to be 100 per cent honest about the products that you are selling; that there can be no hidden ingredients or misleading labelling (such as calling something 'British' food when it was sourced elsewhere and merely packaged in this country); that there should be nothing nasty in the small print, for buyers to discover to their cost later on, like the crafty get-out clauses in certain warranties and insurance policies.

Telling the truth also means acknowledging when things go wrong. It demands that complaints should be handled honestly and fairly (which in turn involves listening to the employee's side of the story too; people rarely invent complaints, but they do tend to exaggerate if they're frustrated and angry). It demands swift action (in my business sales colleagues have the authority to make a decision there and then, rather than having to refer to the manager or head office and so risk a dissatisfied customer feeling that they are being fobbed off). It demands an unambiguous apology free from defensiveness (at Richer Sounds, any customer who writes to me about service, whether good or bad, gets a personalised letter from my office in return). And if a problem is not entirely straightforward it requires a willingness to negotiate a course of action that the customer will find satisfactory. Essentially, it requires a fair answer to the question 'What would you like us to do?'

And this is not an easy thing to sign up to. Confronting the truth can be painful. It forces an organisation to ask itself very blunt questions. Why has this happened? Where did we go wrong? How do we fix it? It also involves facing up to difficult conversations with people who may feel let down or upset.

The fact that truth-telling invariably pays off doesn't, sadly, make organisations any more eager to embrace it. One of the most impressive tales of corporate honesty I know of involves the pharmaceutical company Johnson & Johnson and their bestselling painkiller Tylenol. In the autumn of 1982 it emerged that seven people had died in the Chicago area after taking capsules of Extra-Strength Tylenol that someone had laced with cyanide. Johnson & Johnson's chairman, James Burke, responded immediately, ordering a recall of 31 million bottles of Tylenol capsules from store shelves and offering free replacements in a safer tablet form. He also explained to the media precisely what he was doing. In the immediate wake of the tragedy Johnson & Johnson's share price tumbled, and they also had to set aside $100 million to cover the cost of the recall and replacement. But thanks to James Burke's swift and decisive action, the share price recovered within two months and the company never looked back. It's a textbook example of the power of forthright honesty. The fact, however, that it's still being cited in textbooks thirty-five years after those seven deaths in Chicago suggests to me that James Burke's example is not one that many others have followed.

It's understandable why individuals find it difficult to own up to mistakes. But when it comes to mistakes made by organisations, the situation is made a million times worse by the way most tick. In ones with overbearing management, those first alerted to a potential problem are almost always too scared to say anything about it in case they themselves end up being blamed. In ones with muddled areas of responsibility, people generally buck-pass (which partly goes to explain why governments and bureaucracies are so bad at dealing with crises). Even though history proves again and again that a problem dealt with head on is a problem solved, organisations have a terrible tendency to duck responsibility.

The BA computer system crash in May 2017 is just one recent example of a crisis badly handled. The timing was unfortunate – it was a busy bank holiday weekend – but even allowing for the logistical problems this posed, the company's response was woeful. Almost no information was forthcoming. BA staff were unwilling to communicate with customers, let alone help them. There was no indication that any notice was being taken of the thousands stranded at Heathrow and Gatwick airports – many of whom had to spend the night on the floor. And although the problems started on the Saturday, it wasn't until the Monday that BA's chief executive issued an apology. Even then he was vague both about the cause of the chaos and about passengers' compensation rights. In practical terms it appeared that frontline BA staff were not trained or equipped to deal with the crisis and had no back-up plan. But in cultural terms, I would say that the company had a problem with facing up to hard truths.

As with financial incentives, so openness and honesty in organisations rely on the right triggers. Lying, of course, is hard-wired into our systems – it's reckoned that we start telling lies as young as two. But child psychologists who conducted a simple truth test in which more than 80 per cent of the children lied, found that that figure dropped to 40 per cent if the children were first told that telling the truth was the right thing to do *and* that they would not be punished if they came clean (the figure climbed back to 80 per cent if they were informed that they should tell the truth but would be punished if they had misbehaved). It's not hard to see how that basic principle applies in the world of work, but it's also clear that the culture of many organisations does not embrace it. In poorly run companies, people don't like bad news and the messenger is more than likely to be taken out and shot.

It's not uncommon these days to see corporate values statements that say that whistle-blowing is encouraged. But if you think about it, that's not a great message to put out there. The term 'whistle-blowing' implies that you are asking someone to do something exceptional in which they first have to take a deep breath and then draw attention to themselves. An honest and open company, to my mind, doesn't need whistle-blowers.

And if that sounds utopian, it's worth bearing in mind how the Japanese car manufacturer Toyota pointed the way in the years after the Second World War. Traditionally, car production lines could only be stopped by a whistle-blower in the form of floor manager and he could only blow that whistle to correct a serious mistake (a course of action that usually involved severe consequences for the worker concerned). Such a company philosophy had the inevitable consequence that many cars were produced with faults that had to be corrected further down the line. Then Toyota's Taiichi Ohno introduced a system whereby every worker was given the power to stop the line if a mistake was made or a fault was detected. And if the production line did have to be stopped for any reason, the problem was thrown open to everyone to solve. It's not hard to see how that principle can be more widely applied.

One final obstacle to the idea of the 'self-correcting' company needs to be mentioned – and it's perhaps the biggest of all. As I've already argued, most businesses in competitive sectors ultimately have a choice between doing the right thing by their customers or going to the wall. Sharp practice may take a while to emerge, and the company culture may be such that it proves hard to root out. But ultimately, I do believe that companies that fail to serve their customers well do not last.

What happens, however, when there is no need for that competitive impulse? How does one ensure good behaviour on the part of businesses that operate as virtual monopolies or that are so central to the economy that the direct repercussions to them of bad behaviour are limited or non-existent? Is it possible, for instance, for passengers to be confident of a good train service, given that only one company will operate the rolling stock on any given piece of track? If a bank is too big to be allowed to fail, can its customers be sure that it won't indulge in some form of sharp practice? This is a topic to which I will return later.

CHAPTER 3

NOWT FOR NOWT

THE ENABLERS

EVERY BUSINESS ACKNOWLEDGES, even if it does not always respect, the reciprocal relationship it has with its staff and with its customers. But in any enterprise there's also a third element which, for want of a better word, I would describe as the enablers. In a retail environment these are the people who facilitate the supply chain (drivers and so on), without whom no retailer can exist, and also such support staff as cleaners, lawyers, bankers and the external auditors who check the books. For convenience sake, I would also include the actual suppliers in this category: they are not enablers per se, but the fact that they are not direct employees places them in a not dissimilar relationship to the business as support staff. In a services environment, there may be no supply chain, but there will still be an army of support staff enablers. The public and social sector, too, has its enablers. If you imagine a hospital as a business with employees (the doctors and nurses) and 'customers' (the patients), there will also be an essential army of maintenance people, caretakers, caterers and so on.

In a well-run organisation, the enablers are regarded as an integral part of the whole. It is recognised that they are as essential to the enterprise's success as the other two sides of the business triangle. In badly run concerns, they're often the people who are most neglected and worst treated. But just as I believe that it's the organisations that look after their staff and customers properly that thrive in the long term, so I am convinced that the same principle applies to those organisations that treat their enablers well.

For most people, as I've said before, mention of an ethical treatment of suppliers immediately brings to mind the world of fair trade and green goods. And it's perhaps the most obvious example of the way in which caring for enablers carries material as well as moral benefits. I was fortunate enough to know the late Anita Roddick, who founded The Body Shop in the 1970s, and I developed a huge amount of respect for her. I was also inspired by her basic business philosophy. 'In terms of power and influence, you can forget the church, forget politics,' she once said; 'There is no more powerful institution in society than business, which is why

I believe it is now more important than ever before for business to assume a moral leadership. The business of business should not be about money, it should be about responsibility. It should be about public good, not private greed.'

Anita and her wonderful husband Gordon were tireless campaigners. Gordon was one of the founders of *The Big Issue*, while Anita helped lead the ultimately successful crusade against the testing of cosmetics on animals. In addition she believed in helping communities in the developing world through commerce rather than charity, travelling to Africa and South America to source ingredients for her products and setting up direct links with the small producers so that the benefits fed through to their communities. But ultimately she was an extraordinarily canny businesswoman. Her first shop, which opened in 1976, rapidly became an empire that grew at the rate of 50 per cent a year and that floated successfully on the Stock Exchange in 1984 (the stock was given the nickname 'The shares that defy gravity' because it rose so sharply in value).

Anita probably wasn't a saint – nobody is – but she pointed the way for future fair trade organisations. When Green & Black's founders Craig Sams and Josephine Fairley launched their Maya Gold chocolate, for example, they agreed a five-year rolling contract with the farmers in Belize who supplied the cacao in order to give them a sense of stability and confidence, and paid an advance upfront. 'Until we began trading with the Maya, there was no secondary education for the children from the cacao-growing villages in the rainforest hills,' they recalled later in their book *Sweet Dreams*. Once Maya Gold started rolling off the production line, however, that secondary education became a reality.

Many other companies have followed a similar path. Lush cosmetics, for instance, is careful to buy its raw materials not only in the most environmentally friendly way it can, but at prices that ensure the wellbeing of its suppliers. The company is acutely aware that some of the most expensive ingredients for cosmetics and perfumes come from some of the world's most vulnerable communities. Tea, coffee and many other staples can now be sourced from companies that work closely with the people who grow the raw ingredients.

Critics of such initiatives as fair trade claim that its benefits are limited – that perhaps only a quarter of the extra that shoppers pay for fair trade items actually reaches the farmers and original producers. Some have also suggested that the cost of administering fair trade actually makes Third World producers poorer. I accept that no system is perfect. But although I would be the first to admit that I am not a fair trade expert, the evidence that I have seen persuades me that the advantages for those at what has traditionally been the sharp end of the transaction generally outweigh the disadvantages. Take just one staple, humble food – bananas – of which we in Britain consume over 5 billion a year. According to a report that was prepared for the Corporation for Rural Business Development, banana growers in northern Colombia who joined a Fairtrade-certified scheme found themselves enjoying greater job security, and better access to housing and healthcare. 'All the [hired] workers think that their quality of life with Fairtrade is better,' the report concluded, 'and most think the same about their current economic situation.' This has taken place, it should be added, in a sector of the market where prices have been increasingly squeezed in recent years.

The fair or ethical approach to suppliers has obvious benefits not just for the suppliers themselves but for the other two sides of the retail triangle. Consumers have the comfort of knowing that they are doing something that helps others and protects them from exploitation; they also know that the items they are purchasing are ones that meet their precise requirements – because, say, they involve crops that have not been sprayed with pesticides. The companies benefit from both those considerations, and also from the competitive edge those factors add to their brand.

* *

Today, the number of companies whose stated purpose for existing is fair trade or support of environmental causes, while significant, remains relatively small in terms of the size of the markets that they serve. Back in 2012 the Fairtrade Foundation calculated that fair trade sales in the UK amounted to perhaps £1.57 billion in a year when, according to industry figures, British groceries were turning over £163 billion. The fair trade figure has grown since then, but fair trade turnover still remains a relatively small proportion of the whole. There's an obvious reason for this. Fair trade items tend to be more expensive than their common or garden alternatives, even though with some items that gap is narrowing. For households whose income is squeezed, fair trade can seem a luxury that they cannot afford.

But is it nevertheless possible for businesses as a whole both to operate profitably and deal fairly with those who supply or otherwise serve them? It's very apparent that in highly competitive areas of the market – such as the supermarkets sector – where margins are thin, companies do not always behave well. In 2016 Tesco had to promise to change the way it treated suppliers, after the UK Groceries Code Adjudicator, the supermarkets watchdog, found that they had deliberately and repeatedly withheld money owed to suppliers, so as to boost its sales performance artificially. In one case the supermarket giant had delayed making a multi-million pound payment for more than two years. In a 2015 questionnaire four in ten of Tesco's suppliers claimed that the UK's biggest supermarket failed to comply with the code of practice that governs major retailers' dealings with suppliers.

The price that supermarkets pay for their goods has also come under fire. While the Tesco accounting scandal was rumbling on, farmers were complaining that competition between the various players in the market to be the cheapest sellers of milk was driving the price down to the point where only 20p a litre was being paid for milk that cost 28p to produce. So devastating had been the impact, according to the National Farmers Union, that the number of dairy farms in the UK had actually halved since 2002. Indeed, they pointed out, retailers were selling milk more cheaply than bottled water. Protestors even herded two cows into a branch of Asda to make their point.

On the face of it, it might seem inevitable that in a free market economy, businesses will squeeze suppliers hard in an intensely competitive sector such as food retail. But recent developments suggest that it does not have to be this way. When the Groceries Code Adjudicator published its first statutory review in 2017, it reported that compliance to the code had improved markedly in the handful of years that had elapsed since the Tesco accounting scandal (for example, while a third of suppliers in 2014 had felt that Tesco 'rarely' complied with the code, in 2016 only 6 per cent did). Even more tellingly, a YouGov survey that it commissioned revealed that one of the supermarkets rated best at dealing fairly with its suppliers was one that also prides itself on its very low prices – Aldi. The fact that Aldi should win the approval of 94 per cent of its suppliers, while keeping prices very competitive and increasing its market share at the expense of the other supermarkets, suggests that there is more to the formula of being successful than holding your suppliers down as tightly as you can.

For businesses operating in more niche or specialist areas, there are other, starker considerations. A food supplier might be able to get away with treating a food grower poorly, at least in the short term, because there will be others that they can turn to. But when the nature of your business means that you have comparatively few supply sources to call upon, you have to be considerably more careful. You can't afford to squeeze prices so tightly that a key manufacturer refuses to trade with you: leaving aside the fact that you might end up with nothing to sell, the chances are that that manufacturer will simply move to work more closely with one of your competitors. You also can't afford to see a vital supplier pushed so hard that they end up going out of business. And you can't afford a situation where a supplier reluctantly agrees to carry on working with you but relations are so strained that in an emergency they refuse to go the extra mile for you that is so often required in day-to-day business.

The area of the retail market in which my own company operates is very different from the supermarket sector, but the same basic business principles apply. We too have to compete fiercely on price, and we have to keep a close eye on rivals' prices. But we also know that a race to the bottom never produces a winner. So while we will negotiate hard, we always make sure we end meetings on good terms with our manufacturers. We make sure we pay on time; sometimes we offer early payment, particularly if we know they're having a problem with cash flow.

I happen to think this is good practice, but it's also good business sense. There will be times when we desperately need stock that is in short supply. There will be other times when we want to postpone a repeat delivery because the product hasn't sold as fast as we wanted. We may want help organising a price promotion. We may want to ask if it's possible to get something bespoke to set us apart from our competitors or we may be keen to see if a warranty can be extended. We may have heard that a particular manufacturer is about to offload an end-of-line product at a great price that we know our customers will love, and we want to be at the front of the queue. If our relationship with our suppliers was poor the chances are that they would be more than a little reluctant to help. As it is, we know we can pick up the phone and ask the favour. There's a lot of quid pro quo, and give and take in the area in which I operate, and it invariably works to the two parties' mutual advantage.

I'm acutely aware how difficult it is to pursue this approach all the way down the line. I know that the factory workers who make products for Richer Sounds in China almost certainly don't earn the equivalent to the UK Living Wage (it's a hard calculation to make given the very different cultures and costs of living) and that, as a relatively small player in the vast arena of global electronics, our influence will in any case be limited. But that doesn't mean it's an area of our business we don't need to be concerned with. I've therefore made a point of visiting the Chinese factories that make our products. I have people checking out the workers' dormitories to reassure me that they aren't overcrowded death traps. I've also joined 2,000 other diners in the workers' canteen (rather than the banquet in the directors' dining room which had been prepared for me), all eating standing up at tables, and all going very quiet when we walked in (the soup I had, incidentally, was very nice). These are small steps, I admit, but they are nevertheless important ones.

When it comes to dealing with third parties I often think of the dangers of killing the goose that lays the golden eggs. The food element of that saying suggests to me that the principle applies even in that toughest of sectors – the supermarkets. And, as my Yorkshire friends would say, you get nowt for nowt.

My experience of our Chinese manufacturers was, as I've said, a positive one, but I'm very conscious that this is not always the case. Back in 2010 and 2011, for example, highly critical stories emerged in the media about Foxconn, the firm that produces Apple's iPhones in China. The company, it was said, was forcing its employees to endure 'sweatshop' conditions. At least fourteen employees were believed to have taken their own lives in 2010 alone, most of them by throwing themselves from the company's buildings. The following year the company, which also manufactures for Nintendo, Sony and BlackBerry, installed nets outside some of its factory buildings in Shenzhen in Guangdong Province, to try to control the suicide problem. In 2012 a group of 150 workers gathered on a factory building roof in a Foxconn factory in Wuhan and threatened to jump off. 'The assembly line ran very fast,' one Wuhan worker was reported as saying, 'and after just one morning we all had blisters and the skin on our hand was black. The factory was also really choked with dust and no one could bear it.' There have been further reported problems since.

'The welfare of our employees is our top priority and we are committed to ensuring that all employees are treated fairly,' a Foxconn spokesman said after the 2012 protest. That may well be the case. But what I find particularly striking about the whole Foxconn story is how quickly and widely those initial reports (and follow-up ones) spread around the world. There was a time not that long ago when few in the West would have had much of an inkling what was happening in factories thousands of miles away. But the problems at Foxconn were reported in detail by all the major news outlets, both in print and on television. They were discussed online. Apple itself felt obliged to weigh in. The late Steve Jobs argued that 'We are on top of this.' The company's chief executive, Tim Cook, stated in an interview that Apple were addressing the long hours culture: 'We want everyone to know what we are doing, and we hope that people copy,' he said. 'We've put a ton of effort into taking overtime down.'

In other words, not only did news of alleged problems spread very quickly, but a major customer felt obliged to become involved – it wasn't just Foxconn who made statements and promised to take action. And this leads me on to a further point about the treatment of enablers in any organisational set-up. If there are two carrots dangling that encourage a business's involvement in their welfare – the ethical carrot that states we should treat people as we wish to be treated and the self-interested one that it's in a company's immediate interests to do so – there's also the stick of reputational damage. And thanks to the explosion in online media outlets and discussion forums, that stick has, of late, grown to be a very large one.

Reputational damage has immediate direct effects. Customers will desert a company if it becomes mired in controversy. The organisation may well find itself faced with officially sanctioned penalties or be forced to commit expenditure to putting things right. Its share price or perceived value will almost certainly shrink. It may discover that recruiting becomes that much harder, as able potential employees decide to give it a wide berth. Back in early 2007, before that year's banking crisis, an article in the *Harvard Business Review* on 'Reputation and its Risks' estimated that '70% to 80% of market value comes from hard-to-assess intangible assets such as brand equity, intellectual capital, and goodwill'. Reputational damage, in other words, can be astonishingly costly. Any company worth its salt will strain every muscle to be well regarded by society as a whole.

I'm aware that this may sound rather idealistic. If organisations can be so badly damaged by a scandal that causes a blow to their reputation, a sceptic might argue, why do so many of them continue to take such risks with their good name? And it's certainly true, as the authors of the 'Reputation and its Risk' article argue, that far too many companies focus on crisis management – in other words, in dealing with things after they have gone wrong – rather than on the risk management that would make sure that nothing went wrong in the first place. Nevertheless, although there are still a depressing number of organisations prepared to take short cuts or turn a blind eye to practices that I for one would certainly regard as immoral, I think that the ever-brighter glare of the public spotlight is having an effect. As we know from the commercial success of fair and ethical trade enterprises, customers do care whether the companies they deal with behave well or badly. By the same token, they're likely to vote with their feet if they feel that those companies are betraying their trust.

Take the aftermath of an appalling disaster in one of the most cut-throat sectors of all: clothing. Back in April 2013 the Rana Plaza building, built on swampy ground outside Bangladesh's capital, Dhaka, collapsed suddenly, leaving more than 1,100 workers dead. The subsequent uproar spread round the world. In response to that global criticism action was taken. Safety checks were carried out that led to many factory closures in a country that is the world's second largest exporter of ready-made garments and which supplies such major retailers as Marks & Spencer, Primark and H&M. Working conditions were investigated. It would be naïve to assume, five years after the disaster, that the situation is transformed, but at the very least it's become much harder for UK retailers to close their eyes to the way in which their products are manufactured. Indeed a very interesting new initiative has been launched, backed by the C&A Foundation, that will create a digital map and database of all the clothing factories in Bangladesh. The idea is that such transparency will ultimately improve safety and accountability. It's a worthwhile first step.

Closer to home, fears of reputational harm have led to a tighter focus on a whole swathe of workers who traditionally tended to be ignored: the service staff, such as cleaners and other agency staff, who, often – quite literally – work in the shadows. My view is that, just because they may not be directly employed by the business they serve, that doesn't mean their welfare is not that business's concern. (At Richer Sounds we've actually ended up paying our cleaning agency extra in order to ensure that on our premises their employees earn the Living Wage; when it comes to third-party warehouse staff we've taken steps to ensure that any additional hands taken on at Christmas receive the same.)

So it's encouraging to see that the well-being of such essential staff is starting to become a matter of public concern. In 2015, for example, it emerged that sub-contracted cleaners and security staff at the Department for Environment, Food and Rural Affairs and at HM Revenue & Customs were being paid only £6.50 an hour. Cleaners at the Foreign Office were receiving slightly more – £7.20 an hour, which was the 'national living wage' as of April 2016 – but this still fell far short of the living wage as calculated by the Living Wage Foundation, based on the cost of living in London (£9.15 an hour in 2015, and £10.20 at the time of writing). The scandal predictably led to an outpouring of evasion and buck-passing, but although the outcome did not reflect well on those who should know better, I draw some comfort from the fact that the story did at least receive extensive media coverage. A few years ago, I suspect, few would have known, and even fewer would have cared. I think it's also noteworthy that recent misconduct among some companies in the gig economy sector has not only received media attention but has also had direct repercussions for the companies involved.

We live in a world that is becoming ever more joined up and competitive, where businesses are going to have to fight ever harder for every sale. At the same time it's a world that is becoming more public, where bad behaviour is harder to conceal than it once was and where the scrutiny of bloggers and others is a constant presence. In such an environment I believe that reputation will become an increasingly important element in any organisation's success. I just hope that companies that are tempted to take short cuts with people they don't regard as central to their ongoing prosperity remember the words of Benjamin Franklin: 'It takes many good deeds to build a good reputation, and only one bad one to lose it.'

PART 2

THE ETHICAL CAPITALIST

CHAPTER 4

THE RULES OF THE GAME

FAIR WAGES

I'VE ARGUED SO far that even in purely narrow economic terms ethically run businesses are better businesses – there are huge competitive advantages to be gained from creating an honest and open work culture, from paying a fair wage to ensuring that customers are well treated, and so on. But, as I've also admitted, that demonstrable fact in itself does not, and probably never will, ensure that all businesses operate along those lines. And while I believe that unscrupulous organisations will ultimately meet their comeuppance, this can't mask the harm that they may be doing in the short and medium term.

Unapologetic apologists for capitalism would argue that the occasional malfunction is a price worth paying for a system that has clearly brought considerable benefits to society. Adapting Churchill's remark about democracy – '... it has been said that democracy is the worst form of Government except for all those other forms that have been tried from time to time' – they would also claim that other economic systems are much worse. The fine principles of communism – 'From each according to his abilities, to each according to his needs' – have too often been degraded in practice. Capitalists' proponents view the free market, with its carefully balanced inputs and outputs, as a highly engineered, self-regulating machine. To interfere, in their view, would be like sticking a screwdriver in the works.

I'm not at all convinced by this argument, not least because I think that the machine analogy so often used is a false one. In her book *Doughnut Economics,* Kate Raworth argues that our view of an 'efficient' market is shaped by the misleading images and models that economists have put in our minds. There are the neatly drawn supply and demand curves which meet nicely at the point where price matches supply with demand. There's the famous 'Circular Flow' which brings everything so satisfyingly together: banks taking out income from the system and returning it as investment; government extracting taxes and returning them in the form of public expenditure; overseas traders being paid for goods but also buying goods; and so on. In fact, as she rightly points out, economies in the real world don't work in this satisfyingly clockwork way, and there are also many other factors (from the price of energy to environmental costs) that are crucial to the effective operation of an economy that textbook models invariably ignore. The view that to modify the system to deal with any potential shortcomings is to destroy a well-oiled machine therefore simply doesn't stand up. The well-oiled machine never existed in the first place, outside the minds of a few true believers and theorists.

The fact is, too, that even if 'pure' capitalism ever actually existed, it's long disappeared. Within a matter of decades of the start of the industrial revolution in Britain, governments (under pressure from trades unions and philanthropists) felt the need to intervene to improve the appalling working conditions in factories. They realised that they couldn't simply leave things to individual factory owners. The America of the so-called 'Gilded Age', with its handful of wealthy plutocrats, was similarly short-lived and had disappeared long before the First World War. Gradually the ten- or twelve-hour day gave way to the eight-hour day, despite the claims of employers that the first eleven hours put in by workers merely covered the factory's overheads and that any profit appeared only in the last hour. Paid holidays made an appearance, child labour was stopped, health regulations were brought in, often thanks again to pressure from trades unions. The 1980s may have seen a resurgence in free market liberalism, whereby some restrictions were lifted, workers' rights were undermined and taxes lowered in the vague hope that the increased wealth accruing to the minority would somehow 'trickle down' to everyone else. But even then there was no suggestion that all controls and regulations should be consigned to the waste-paper bin. Today, no one who espouses an entirely free market actually lives in one, even if the years of deregulation led to a certain mission creep – or rather 'capitalism creep'.

So it's very important to avoid the narrow view that you either buy into off-the-peg capitalism and accept its faults, or you don't have capitalism. And that requires quite a major mind shift for many. I'm reminded of the arguments that raged in Britain back in the late 1970s and early 1980s when it was first suggested that people in cars should be legally obliged to wear seat belts. The practical wisdom of this was irrefutable – nearly 6,000 people a year were dying in car accidents at the time. But for the large number who opposed this move, it seemed an unjustifiable assault on the fundamental principle of individual freedom (the same people also tended to support the notion that one should be allowed to drink and drive). In the event, legislation was passed and today, with many more cars on the road than thirty-odd years ago, the annual number of fatalities has fallen to well under 2,000. Nobody thinks twice now about buckling up, and if asked about it they would, I suspect, couch the discussion in terms of social responsibility rather than libertarian principles.

For me, capitalism is a bit like a car. It does wonderful things, but it's also potentially lethal. Adopting a few safety measures won't reduce our ability to go where we want when we want. But such measures are nevertheless of paramount importance.

Central to all this is the issue of wages. In Part 1 I argued that not only is paying at the very least the Living Wage the right thing to do, but businesses that adopt it can and do operate profitably. To my mind government legislation in this area is entirely legitimate. Since, however, it's such an emotive topic among purist promoters of the free market, it's perhaps worth exploring in a little more detail.

The case against a minimum wage is a simple one: it reduces levels of employment. If, the argument goes, you're operating your business with ten members of staff whom you pay £5 an hour, but are then forced to pay each of them £10 an hour, you will need to get rid of half the workforce in order to keep your profits at their previous level. You could, of course, take the alternative route of putting up your prices, but if you do that the end result will be much the same. Higher prices mean that you sell less, and if you sell less you will be back to employing fewer people or using machines.

Given the iron logic of this, it comes as no surprise that when a national minimum wage of £3.60 an hour was introduced in Britain in 1999, dire warnings were issued by a large number of business leaders and economists. But what was the actual result? Unemployment fell, and continued to do so for the next few years even as the minimum wage started to edge upwards. It took the financial crash of 2008 (which, of course, had nothing to do with the minimum wage) to reverse the trend. Today, unemployment is lower than it was in 2000, and the living wage is scheduled to rise further.

The goal set by the Low Pay Commission is that the living wage should reach 60 per cent of median earnings by 2020. The Living Wage Foundation (LWF), seeking among other things to offset the discrimination against the under 25s encapsulated in the government scheme, is more ambitious, making its calculations on actual living costs (which is why it recommends a higher rate for a very expensive city such as London). Theirs is a voluntary scheme, but it's one that 3,800 employers, including such giants as Nestlé and Aviva and smaller players such as Richer Sounds, have so far signed up to. One way and another, a third of FTSE 100 companies pay LWF rates not just to their directly employed staff but to the employees of their contractors (provided these work on the employers' premises for at least two hours a day for a period of eight consecutive weeks).

So why hasn't the introduction of a degree of wage regulation had the disastrous impact it should theoretically have done? There's no one simple answer to this, but it does seem that the economic law of higher wages = fewer jobs is not as iron-cast as has been traditionally stated. Yes, a minimum wage (certainly according to research in the US) can lead to some unemployment, particularly among unskilled workers in sectors where automation has taken hold. But since what people are paid in a capitalist society is down to a broad range of factors (skill, demand, bargaining power, and also such hard-to-measure factors as perceived prestige), wages have never been arrived at by the precise economic formula that some have suggested.

Nor has employment itself ever been the efficiently frictionless system some would like to claim. You can't switch it on and off like an electrical switch, according to demand: people may not hang around waiting for the lights to come back on, and so key skills may have been lost by the time power is restored. And the idea that it's easy to move to wherever the jobs are is a nonsense. Former Conservative minister Norman Tebbit may have famously talked of his father having 'got on his bike and looked for work', but it's not so easy to do that if you have family commitments where you live, if your children are happy at their current school, or if you've built up a local network of friendship and support. Of course, industry patterns do change and if the factory or pit in a town closed thirty years ago, there comes a point when people have no choice but to search for alternative employment elsewhere. Populations do move, towns expand and contract. But these are not easy processes for people, particularly in an era when there is almost no social housing, and it can take many years to obtain. Again, all this leads to bumps and irregularities in the structure of people's wages and prevents them from being rationally determined by 'the market'.

When considering the case for the minimum wage (or rather, in my view, the Living Wage Foundation's calculation of what the minimum wage should be), it's also worth bearing in mind the various economic advantages that it leads to. Higher wages can act as an incentive for people to work harder, and so improve a company's productivity. They can encourage people to take work rather than fall back on benefits. By putting more money in employees' pockets, they simultaneously help boost consumer spending. According to a study carried out in 2017 by the Cardiff Business School, companies that had signed up to the Living Wage did so for reputational reasons, 86 per cent of them saying that their involvement had enhanced their organisation's standing, and more than half reported that it had improved relations between staff and managers, increased the commitment and motivation of Living Wage employees and improved recruitment to those lower paid jobs. Only a handful reported finding it necessary to claw back costs by reducing jobs, hours or employee benefits.

Intervention, then, has not destroyed some delicately balanced mechanism. Instead, I would argue, a degree of regulation has not only helped address an unfair imbalance, but has created benefits – both for individual employees and for society more widely.

This basic principle of justified intervention needs to be borne in mind as one considers the interrelated employment problems Britain currently faces. On the one hand, we've become a country with high levels of employment but relatively low levels of productivity. On the other, our high levels of employment have generally come from areas of the jobs market that are low-skilled and low-paid. On the one hand, we lag significantly behind countries such as France, Germany, Belgium and the Netherlands in the productivity league table. On the other, we have a workforce full of poorly paid people with low skills levels and little access to the training that would help them improve their lot.

Two particular manifestations of the low-wage economy have become increasingly marked in recent years. The first is the zero-hours contract. For some people, admittedly, it has its benefits. It allows them greater flexibility over how many hours they work and when, enabling them to take on more than one job. But it also comes with significant drawbacks, and when it's effectively forced on an employee I think it's utterly immoral. Although in theory a zero-hours contract allows the individual to turn down work, this can prove far harder to do in practice. A contract of this type offers no fixed income and none of the benefits such as sick pay and holiday pay that most employees regard as standard. Among other things, such instability makes it impossible to get a loan or a mortgage or even rent a property in the private sector.

The online-driven gig economy, involving independent workers on short-term engagements, comes with similar advantages for some and drawbacks for many. If you're a highly skilled self-employed professional, such as a graphic designer or an electrician, who is looking for a new way to work as a freelance, it can offer fantastic opportunities by linking you up with potential clients you might otherwise never have come across. If you're a delivery driver, on the other hand, while it may offer you flexible working hours, it may also come with the massive disadvantages of low pay and no contractual benefits.

According to the Office for National Statistics, the number of people on zero-hours contracts more than trebled between 2012 and 2017. What's more, such contracts spread not only in traditionally insecure areas of the market like hotels and restaurants, but even made inroads into previously untouched sectors such as higher education, where some universities started to employ junior lecturers on this basis. By the end of 2017, 883,000 workers were reported to be on zero-hours contracts. While some may have said that they were happy with the flexibility these contracts gave them, 42 per cent said that they were dissatisfied, that they were keen to earn more than they were currently receiving, but that they felt there was little they could do to improve their situation. The number of those reckoned to be involved in some version (both good and bad) of the gig economy in Britain in 2018 stands at about 5 million, according to the McKinsey Global Institute, though many of these will be well-paid skilled workers. Overall, the TUC has calculated that if current trends continue, 3.5 million people in the UK could be in insecure work by 2022.

I'm not pretending that there are quick-fix solutions to the low-wage end of the economy. But I don't accept that one has to accept poor pay as a necessary or inevitable element of a modern economy. In fact I would argue the opposite. Low wages have bad economic effects as well as terrible social outcomes. They create a self-perpetuating system in which poor pay leads to low skills, low morale, low productivity, lack of training and high labour turnover, leading back to poor pay. An investigation into the effects of the national living wage by the Institute for Public Policy Research noted that Britain's low wage sectors – agriculture, retail and hotels and restaurants – employ a third of all workers, and produce 23 per cent of the UK's gross value added. But on average they are 29 per cent less productive than the economy as a whole. Poor pay is worsening our pretty terrible productivity record: it's not helping it. In Germany, by contrast, where workers take about 4.5 days to achieve what British workers manage in 5, wages in virtually every sector are higher.

The Taylor Review on modern working practices, which was commissioned by the government and came out in 2017, has an excellent term for the world of the gig economy: 'one-sided flexibility'. In an employment situation where there is two-way flexibility, it explains, people choose a non nine-to-five way of working, or a low-hours contract, because it suits their life and it suits the employer. One-sided flexibility, by contrast, involves employers seeking 'to transfer all risk on to the shoulders of workers, in ways which make people more insecure and make their lives harder to manage'.

To tackle this, the Taylor Review suggests various steps need to be taken. The Low Pay Commission should encourage the government to introduce a new minimum wage for those on zero-hours contracts and people should have the right to request a fixed number of working hours from their employers. More transferable skills should be taught to workers. And the notion should be accepted of a 'dependent contractor' who 'is not an employee, but neither are they genuinely self-employed' who enjoy the status and protection of regular employment – for example, they would receive sick pay and holiday leave.

The TUC – and I would agree with it – have argued that the Taylor Review simply doesn't go far enough. In the TUC's view there should be an outright ban on zero-hours contracts: people working regular hours should have the right to a guaranteed-hours contract and should receive overtime pay for hours outside of their contracts. There should be a written statement of terms, conditions and working hours, from day one. Agency workers should be entitled to the going rate for the job, on an equal basis with directly employed workers, not least to stop employers trying to take exploitative short cuts.

Whatever is finally decided upon – and I for one believe that urgent action is essential – it will need much more than just legislation or a government expression of intent if it is to have any real effect. All legislation contains loopholes that the unscrupulous will exploit (in this area the whole question of who is and isn't self-employed, and what employers can gain from classing workers as self-employed, is very complex in legal and tax terms). And legislation that doesn't involve subsequent monitoring and close scrutiny simply gets ignored.

I have depressing direct experience of this. Back in 2012 the then Home Secretary Theresa May introduced a measure to compel agencies to respond to persistent anti-social behaviour. Four years later, a small charity I set up, ASB Help, which supports people victimised by anti-social behaviour, investigated this so-called 'Community Trigger' and found that, although much needed and well meaning, it had been given no publicity or resources. The result? Most local authorities seemed unaware of it. 'In many cases, we would suggest it is nothing more than a bureaucratic exercise, creating more paperwork, draining already tight public resources, and yet still not bringing desperately-needed respite for victims,' a spokesperson from ASB Help concluded.

Any legislation in the low-pay and zero-hours arena, then, will need to be backed up by considerably more than goodwill. There's no point in creating rules but not holding people to them: it's like having a football match without a referee. At the same time, I believe that real change only tends to take place when it involves reputation as much as it does compliance. Those companies that have signed up to the Living Wage have done so in part because they believe it is the right thing to do, and in part because they are concerned how they will be regarded by employees, prospective employees and their customers if they don't. If you want people to alter their behaviour, you have to make them feel that their current attitudes are out of step with the times: you have to literally shame them. Once they are embarrassed about the way they are behaving, they will observe rules that otherwise they would be using all their ingenuity to bypass

A focus on the relationship between employer and employee is, of course, at the heart of the whole low-pay debate, but it's not the only factor that should be borne in mind. The other major consideration is the huge social costs that low pay involves. We tend to assume that unemployment poses the big financial problem for the country's workforce. But today there's also a major issue with underpaid underemployment (according to the Institute for Fiscal Studies one in five low-paid men is working less than a thirty-hour week). One might expect, for instance, that child poverty will only be found in those families where the responsible adult or adults are not in work. Yet, according to the Child Poverty Action Group, two-thirds of children growing up in poverty – some 3 million all told – live in a family where at least one person has a job.

The repercussions of this are numerous. The TUC has calculated that growth of insecure employment (in other words, working without guaranteed hours or baseline employment rights) costs the Exchequer around £4 billion a year in lost income tax and National Insurance contributions. Then there's the multi-billion-pound cost of the tax credits system which Gordon Brown introduced as a way to lift people out of poverty (but which has been used by the more unscrupulous employers as a means to pay less to their employees). Not to mention the public expense of other welfare payments which poorer members of society are entitled to and which they desperately need.

But it's the price exacted on the individual that is the highest. Poor people lead shorter, more unhealthy lives than their more prosperous neighbours. They are more likely to be the victims of violent crime. Research suggests, too, that they are up to twice as likely to suffer from mental ill-health. Even if you were hard-hearted enough to regard people merely as a resource, you would have to accept that such outcomes represent a shockingly wasteful use of that resource.

If wage poverty in Britain has been on the rise in recent years, so has social inequality. Indeed there's a clear, though not absolutely in-step, link between the two. And just as low incomes exact a heavy price on the individual and society, so, I believe, do the gaping disparities that have grown up between the rich and the poor.

Wealth inequality has, of course, been with us for centuries, not to say millennia. In the UK it narrowed in the era of the First World War through a combination of high taxes on the rich and full employment, widened again before the Second World War and then reduced again. By 1979 the top 10 per cent were taking just over 20 per cent of UK income, while the poorest 10 per cent had around 4 per cent. But since then the gap has grown massively again. By 2010 the top 10 per cent were getting more than a 30 per cent share (double that of the next richest 10 per cent), while the share for the poorest 10 per cent had dwindled to around 1 per cent. Today, according to the Institute for Fiscal Studies, when it comes to individual wealth, more than half in the UK is held by only 10 per cent of households. Those who can't afford to own their own house not only own virtually no capital, but usually have few or no savings and inadequate pensions and often have to cope with sizeable personal debt.

To my mind, as long as hard work can be seen to bring direct rewards, a degree of inequality can be a good motivator. I would therefore agree with Professor Branko Milanović of the City University of New York, who endeavours to ascertain 'what types of inequalities may be good for growth (for example, inequality due to differential effort) and what are not (inequality due to gender, race or parental wealth)' – although I think one would have to acknowledge that 'differential effort' is not a level playing field: if it was, mothers – who work very long hours – would be among the wealthiest of all. The problem, in my view, arises when at one end wealth speeds up and becomes self-generating (through income generated by rising property prices and investments, for example) and at the other end poverty becomes a self-reinforcing cycle. 'A rising tide lifts all boats,' John F. Kennedy once said. That's clearly not the case today.

From a narrow economic point of view, neither of the extremes in a very unequal society is good for business. Those at the bottom won't be in a position to spend their money confidently and so support the consumer economy; those at the very top rarely spend in line with the rate they earn and are more likely than not to park their money unproductively in the Cayman Islands.

But inequality is also deeply pernicious. As Richard Wilkinson and Kate Pickett demonstrate in their book *The Spirit Level,* it breaks down social cohesion; it leads to shorter and unhealthier lives; it increases rates of teenage pregnancy, violence, obesity, crime and addiction. Whether or not inequality is always bad for the *whole* of society is arguably not quite as clear-cut as Wilkinson and Pickett claim: in some areas – infant mortality is one – their thesis does seem to hold water (in unequal Britain, death rates among the wealthy are higher than among the poorest in more equal Sweden); in other areas of daily life – literacy, for instance – the children of the better-off tend to score better regardless of how equal the society in which they live is. Nevertheless, inequality certainly exacerbates social problems and individual unhappiness. Recent events (and common sense) suggest that it can contribute to political instability, too.

If there is a powerful social and economic argument for intervening to raise wages at the bottom, is there also one for controlling levels of remuneration at the top?

Because most of us focus on what affects us directly, we tend to worry less about perceived wage inequality when times are good because the chances are that we will be benefiting, too. But when times are more challenging, as they certainly have been for the past decade, and many are seeing their incomes stagnate or even reduce, pay inequality understandably becomes a burning issue.

The case for letting pay at the top level take its own course is, essentially, very much the same as the one for not intervening to adjust low wages: the market knows best and rewards accordingly. If the supply of top executives and brilliant entrepreneurs is limited – as I think it would be fair to say that it is – then demand for them will inevitably drive their price up. At the same time, there is no question but that good CEOs and senior staff have a huge impact on the success of the companies they run. They may be very well paid but then they are simultaneously adding value and profit to the enterprises for which they are responsible.

To my mind, this is fine as far as it goes, and it would be hypocritical of me as someone who strongly believes in rewarding success to argue differently. But the problem is that just as the market for lower paid workers is neither as frictionless nor as free from distortion as classic economic doctrine would suggest, so pay at the top is often shaped by forces that have nothing to do with the simple economic questions of supply and demand, or with the qualitative issue of individual excellence.

City pay offers the classic instance of this. Once upon a time, most bankers earned salaries that were comparable to other well-paid professions, such as doctors and lawyers. Those who commanded high levels of reward tended to be those who were partners in merchant banks (or investment banks, as they are now called) who did so because they were staking their own cash and so stood to lose out if things went wrong, just as they benefited when times were good. In other words, they had 'skin in the game'.

With increasing deregulation in the 1970s and 1980s, however, since many investment banks chose to float on the markets as public companies, that direct link between performance and reward was lost. Pay and bonuses rose inexorably regardless of success or failure. At the height of the banking crisis in 2007 and 2008 top executives were continuing to be financially rewarded just as the government was embarking on a rescue programme that would see £1,162 billion of taxpayers' money – £17,838 for every man, woman and child in the UK – being pumped in in the form of cash and guarantees to save their institutions. Rewards for risks taken or results achieved had become rewards regardless of outcome.

Today, it's not just financial institutions that tick this way. Time and time again, we see companies that are struggling run by a board that is raking in cash for itself. The chief executive of construction firm Carillion was paid more than £500,000 in bonuses in 2017, even though the company was deeply in debt and staggering towards collapse.

This is bad enough, but it gives rise to an additional problem: once you have a culture of high pay whatever the circumstances, it becomes self-reinforcing. Pay rarely goes down. Instead remuneration committees level up to what they believe the 'market rate' to be, advised by members who are often directors of other companies, and supported by corporate head hunters whose salary-based commission can hardly be said to make them disinterested bystanders. Organisations persuade themselves that they're in a frantic battle for 'talent' that either won't come to them because they're not offering enough or is planning to leave them because a competitor is offering more. Hence the suggestion by some during the BBC pay disclosure controversy that there is a cut-throat international market for our British newsreaders. I for one find that hard to believe.

The fact that arguments over high pay are now breaking out in sectors that have never previously witnessed them shows just how badly things have got out of kilter. The recent dispute concerning the payment of vice chancellors at British universities is a case in point. Research by Times Higher Education in 2017 suggested that while pay for rank-and-file academic staff had dropped in real terms by 2.8 per cent in the five years since 2011/12 when tuition fees had been raised to £9,000, the average vice chancellor's had risen by 15 per cent. Pay for many top executives in other walks of life – local government, for example – has similarly accelerated as rewards for those further down the pecking order have stalled.

All the arguments used to defend high rewards in traditionally well-rewarded sectors are now unquestioningly deployed to defend the new status quo at the top. 'Pay peanuts and you get monkeys' is the classic one, begging the question whether, in the case of university vice chancellors, those previously doing the job on lower salaries were deemed at the time to be not that good but the best that could be found for the money. 'It's an international market for talent' is another, raising the question again (as with people on low pay) just how fluid the labour market really is (a quick check of current British university vice chancellors reveals only a handful born and educated outside the UK). 'It's comparable to what people in X industry are getting' is perhaps the least convincing justification of all, since it ignores the very basic truth that people's choice of careers and professions is influenced by their interests and skills and not just by money considerations. It's tempting to respond to a vice chancellor or the head of a local council or the CEO of a company who says, 'I could have been an investment banker' with the question, 'Why weren't you one, then?'

Such arguments in defence of unconditional high pay also ignore the astonishingly corrosive effects it can have on the proper functioning and future success of an organisation. If the people at the top are rewarding themselves while holding pay rises for others at bay, morale suffers. Brand image can come under attack, too, as is apparent from the recent controversy surrounding the high bonuses announced at house builder Persimmon (not least because it was the government's help-to-buy scheme, introduced in 2013, rather than the company's own efforts, that was largely responsible for Persimmon's financial success and that therefore made the chief executive's £110 million bonus possible). The bonus culture can lead to poor decisions, as senior executives agree on business strategies or company mergers that flatter the share price but damage the long-term health of the company.

I accept that regulating pay at the top is far from straightforward. Calculating a minimum wage involves measurable factors, such as the cost of living. There may be different views as to what constitutes a *reasonable* standard of living (hence, in part, the reason for the gap between the national living wage and the Living Wage), but it's possible, by looking at the average cost of rent, food and so on, to come up with a basic figure. But how do you decide when a lot is too much? For that matter, how do you determine which jobs are intrinsically worth more than others? If a group of people found themselves marooned on a desert island and forced to start a new society, the ones whose skills were most needed in the short term would almost certainly be the farmers, doctors, builders, mothers and teachers. The tax barristers and investment bankers would find themselves in rather less demand except, possibly, as unskilled labour. And even among that former group of essential workers it would be very tricky to put a value on factors such as relative skill, perceived social importance and unsociable working hours.

Since, as I've already said, I believe that a degree of inequality in society is unfortunately unavoidable, I don't think for a moment that the answer to this conundrum is to lower top pay to some arbitrary level or to set official rates for different sectors. But since I also believe that reward at the top should be closely linked to success, I would argue that high pay has to be accountable. That it's clearly not at present is starkly revealed in two depressing numbers supplied by the chartered financial analysts' body CFA UK in 2016: over the previous thirteen years, they reported, the wage packets of FTSE 350 chief executives had risen by 82 per cent. In the same period the return on money invested in those companies had climbed by 1 per cent.

Britain has traditionally been very secretive about executive remuneration. Scandinavian countries, by contrast, have long had a culture of transparency, the relevant authorities in Sweden, Finland and Norway annually putting everyone's income tax returns in the public domain. 'The British seem not to mind being watched by millions of surveillance cameras, but they do not want their salaries to be public record,' the *Financial Times* reported; 'In Sweden it is the other way around.' It seems to me no coincidence that pay for corporate executives in Sweden is lower than in the UK, and that there is no bonus culture. Barclays Bank, for example, is, according to Reuters, twice the size of Sweden's Swedbank, but its chief executive is paid twenty-three times as much as Swedbank's. Needless to add: Swedish companies perform just as well, if not better, for their shareholders as British ones do.

So I think that in the interests of the fairness that should lie at the heart of all business, full disclosure is an important first step. As the BBC's recent experience has shown, it will not lead to a mass poaching of talented people by other organisations, nor will it lead to wage inflation to counter that potential mass poaching (in fact, in the BBC's case, several highly paid individuals actually took wage cuts in response to the public furore). And it will create greater transparency and fairness within the organisation (among other things, bringing pay of men and women into line with one another and ensuring that there is no discrimination on ethnic grounds).

Moreover, the reputational implications entailed in disclosure will put greater pressure on remuneration committees to take a tougher line. As the American lawyer Louis Brandeis once put it: 'Publicity is justly commended as a remedy for social and industrial diseases. Sunlight is said to be the best of disinfectants; electric light the most efficient policeman.' I think it would also be beneficial if other stakeholders – employees and trades unionists – sat on those committees and had a vote. At the very least, they would serve as a useful counterbalance to the institutional shareholders whose concern is with immediate dividends and share price rather than the long-term health of a business.

One rule of thumb route I favour would be to establish a transparent ratio of top- to bottom-end salaries within an organisation, which could be debated and agreed by that organisation's stakeholders. When the TUC looked at this in 2014, it found that across the FTSE 100 companies, the mean ratio of highest paid director total earnings to average employee pay was 138:1 (to the national living wage it was 293:1). Bearing in mind the less than impressive impact that rising rates of executive pay have had on company growth which I touched on earlier, these ratios are surely excessive and impossible to justify. (Just to be clear, I am talking about multiples of salary here; I have no problem with business people who have risked their own capital receiving a dividend as a reward for success.)

The other key element in take-home pay is, of course, tax, and it's to that topic that I turn next.

CHAPTER 5

CAPITALISM AND THE COMMUNITY

PAYING TAXES

IN AN INTERVIEW with *Women's Own* magazine in 1987, the then prime minister Margaret Thatcher outlined what she felt the relationship between the individual and the community to be. 'There's no such thing as society,' she said. 'There are individual men and women and there are families.'

For many of us around then, Thatcher's controversial comment came to symbolise the individualistic spirit of the 1980s: people are successful through their own hard work, the mood seemed to suggest; they shouldn't feel any obligation to the people around them. Today this kind of 'me first' attitude seems to be even more deeply embedded. Take the title of a recent article published by the American business magazine *Inc.*: 'Why Selfishness Is a Virtue'.

But Margaret Thatcher was wrong. There *is* such a thing as society. We all need people around us who can provide the support and services that make everyday life possible – we all benefit from a complex web of social relationships that extends far beyond our families and friends. Even the supposedly narrow world of business, with its focus on profitability and the bottom line, relies heavily on the community. It may look to individuals for its customers, but it needs society as a whole to provide its employees and to create and maintain the infrastructure without which it cannot possibly survive. Business people who say that they've succeeded completely on their own can only ever be right up to a point. They may have created their venture from scratch, or have taken an existing one and built it up, but those enterprises will be deeply dependent on the community and cannot flourish without it.

When that community infrastructure isn't there or doesn't work as well as it might, it's businesses who are among the first to notice and to complain. To take just a single example: one contributory factor to Britain's disappointing productivity record (which I outlined briefly in Chapter 4) is its poor broadband service, which is reckoned by many to be among the worst in Europe. Successive governments have hoped that individual broadband providers would take up the slack, but it's clear that the investment required is far greater than those providers are prepared to put in. There are direct business consequences, and business looks to the wider community to help fund the service via the taxes it pays. In 2017 the government therefore made some funds available in the form of a share of the £500 million it committed to the technology sector in its latest National Productivity Investment Fund review. It's clearly nothing like enough, but it shows an acceptance of the principle that broadband has now become so central to the effective functioning of both individual businesses and the broader economy that government has to play its part in building and maintaining it.

In longer-established parts of the country's physical infrastructure this community involvement is, of course, taken for granted. Transport demonstrates this particularly clearly. Although, historically, many roads were privately built and maintained – as were all railways – road and railway infrastructure have long been publicly funded. In 2016–17 alone the government spent almost £30 billion on everything from repairing potholes to upgrading track. In the same period nearly 153 billion tonnes of domestic freight was carried on Britain's roads, and £5.9 billion's worth of economic output was supported via the railways. Essential commercial activity, in other words, was possible thanks only to government spending. Roads and railways are the arteries of business. When someone tells me that they're a 'self-made' millionaire, I'm tempted to ask them how they got into work that morning.

As with the built infrastructure of the country, so with the UK's intellectual infrastructure. It's not businesses that teach their staff the three Rs. Nor is it businesses that pay for the higher levels of academic skills that are now becoming ever more essential in an increasingly competitive world. Yet it's the government-funded education that accounts for 93 per cent of Britain's workforce that provides all the basics that every employer needs, that raises people's productivity and creativity, and promotes entrepreneurship and technical expertise. And while there is no proven correlation between the *amount* of education a country such as Britain offers and its economic achievements, there is plenty of evidence to suggest a link between high-quality education and economic success. It's not surprising, then, that corporate bodies are endlessly lobbying government to invest in STEM (science, technology, engineering and maths) education – they're very aware that a well-educated workforce results in more successful and profitable companies.

If businesses rely on government to support their endeavours, they also expect it to take up the slack where they are unable or unwilling to do so – in cleaning up the environment after them, for example, or in making up the shortfall for those on low pay.

Billions are spent each year to fight industrial pollution. Billions are dedicated to the payment of benefits (and in effectively subsidising businesses via tax credits). A proportion of the funding required for such expenditure obviously comes from businesses in the form of corporation tax, business rates and so on, but much is drawn directly from the pockets of individual tax payers via income tax (27 per cent of tax receipts in 2015–16), VAT (18 per cent of tax receipts) and so on. Business, in other words, picks up only part of the tab.

There's a wider point to be made here, too. The state doesn't just help enterprise by spending taxes on essential services like roads and schools. It also creates the economic environment in which it is possible to do business in the first place. We're often told that capitalism is about buying and selling in a realm completely free from government interference: the fabled 'free market'. What this story ignores is that, as I suggested in Chapter 4, these exchanges are possible only thanks to government regulation. From maintaining the money supply and issuing banknotes, right through to creating the legal basis for contracts and private property, the state is in the background of every business transaction. If I buy a loaf of bread, the shopkeeper is only happy to accept a £1 coin because he or she knows that the state and society recognises that it's worth something – and I'm only happy to take it because I know that, if the loaf isn't up to scratch, the law would be on my side when I asked for a refund. The Cambridge economist Ha-Joon Chang summarises this point pithily, arguing that there's 'no such thing' as an exchange that's completely free of regulation: 'If some markets *look* free it is only because we so totally accept the regulations that are propping them up that they become invisible,' he says. It's yet another demonstration of the fact that at every stage of doing business, business people need the state and the community it represents.

How have we reached the point where so many in the corporate world think they owe nothing to society? Organisations have, of course, pursued self-interested agendas for as long as business has been around, even though they have often claimed the opposite. The Bank of England was set up in 1694 with a remit to 'promote the public good and benefit of our people'. Over 200 years later, in the 1920s, Walter Leaf, the chairman of Westminster Bank Ltd, wrote that the strength of British banks was mainly down to 'the sense that Directors have conducted the business of their banks with constant attention to public interests in the first place'. There may have been an underlying philosophy that there was a reciprocal relationship between the corporate world and the public, even if that ideal was rarely lived up to.

There has, however, been a sea change over the past few decades. Previously, companies at least paid lip service to the idea of the public good. But during the 1970s a shift began towards an openly more selfish, individualistic theory of business. And as with most of the big changes that have taken place in capitalism over the last century, it started in the US. A number of economists, for the most part based at the University of Chicago, put forward a radical new set of ambitions they said businesses should adopt, ambitions that were perhaps most succinctly summarised by their foremost spokesman, Milton Friedman. 'There is one and only one social responsibility of business – to use its resources and engage in activities designed to increase its profits,' he wrote in an article first published in the *New York Times* magazine in 1970. Managers who pursued anything other than profit were, in his view, 'unwitting puppets of the intellectual forces that have been undermining the basis of a free society these past decades'. Ultimately, he argued, the only obligation that any business had was to its shareholders.

At first, Friedman and his followers' ideas were seen as unreasonable, and even dangerous. But gradually, they became the norm – first in America, and then around the world. By 2004, the renowned management guru Peter Drucker was able to summarise the new spirit of capitalism in the following blunt words: 'If you find an executive who wants to take on social responsibilities, fire him, fast.'

The ruthless pursuit of shareholder value, however, is not actually a company's legal obligation. What's more, it is downright dangerous. If managers believe that their duty is only to their shareholders – and not at all to society more generally – they will be prepared to make socially harmful decisions in pursuit of immediate gain. In one particularly troubling study from 2007, reported in the *Journal of Business Ethics*, in which researchers surveyed thirty-four high-level American company directors about their priorities, it emerged that thirty-one would cut down a mature forest or release a dangerous, unregulated toxin into the environment if they thought it would improve their company's profits. And this isn't just some theoretical problem. Time and time again, companies have been shown to have taken dangerous short cuts to make money. One journalist who investigated the causes of the Deepwater Horizon disaster, the largest oil spill in US waters in history, linked the disaster with oil company BP's tendency to 'encourage managers to put short-term financial goals ahead of the long-term health of the business and its employees'.

But what's perhaps most shocking about the obsession with profit is that it doesn't even serve the interests of the companies themselves. It's self-evident: if you're directing all your attention to the bottom line for the next quarter, you're not going to make decisions that serve the long-term interests of your company. Sadly, 'short-termism' is now built into the mindset of managers. When the management consultants McKinsey ran a survey of Canadian business people, they found that nearly 80 per cent of top executives felt under pressure to prioritise their businesses' financial performance over two years or less; only 7 per cent said they were encouraged to think about the five-year performance of their organisation.

The impact of the Chicago School approach to business has been twofold. It's made individual companies more prone to take short-term risks at the cost of long-term stability. And it's made the global economy as a whole more volatile and less able to achieve consistent growth. A study of one American stock index, the S&P 500, by the economist Roger Martin, found that during the 'golden age' when managers were less focused on profits alone (approximately the years 1933–76), the annual return on stocks was actually *higher* than in more recent times (1976–2011) when profit was prioritised above all else. The fact is that, leaving the rest of society out of the equation for a moment, conscienceless capitalism doesn't work even for the shareholders.

Admittedly, since the 2007 financial crash, the obsession with shareholders' profit has come in for some long-overdue criticism. Jack Welch, the former CEO of General Electric, famously described it as 'the dumbest idea in the world'. And there has been a recent resurgence in the idea of 'corporate social responsibility', with companies taking on philanthropic projects so they can give something back to society. But unfortunately, most businesses still have a long way to go. I think it doesn't help that shareholders are often so far removed from the company in which they have invested. Distance encourages indifference. There's nothing like having to experience face to face the consequences of decisions you have allowed or pushed for to make you question future decisions a little more closely.

There's one very obvious way in which businesses *can* give back to the community. The problem is, they usually put a lot of effort into finding ways to avoid it. I'm talking, of course, about tax. These days, it feels like you can't move for stories about people trying to find ever more ingenious ways to avoid paying their tax bill – whether they're giant tech firms like Facebook or wealthy individuals such as TV celebrities or major landowners.

Many business people argue that tax avoidance is entirely justifiable. Eric Schmidt, the former chief executive of Google, has said he is 'very proud' of his company's tax-avoiding structure. 'It's called capitalism,' he said. 'We are proudly capitalistic.' And they construct various ingenious justifications for their tax avoidance stance in particular and for low-tax economies in general.

One particularly popular argument is that if tax rates are 'too high', or if governments attempt to collect them too aggressively, the rich will simply move to a low-tax environment. In the words of US politician Chris Christie, 'If you tax them, they will leave.' It's a superficially plausible view, as is the argument that follows from it: that tax revenues in high-tax countries will inevitably fall because the rich have left. It's not a view, however, that is borne out by the facts. Some 84 per cent of those who featured on Forbes' 2017 list of the world's billionaires still live in the country of their birth. Only 5 per cent moved abroad after they had become successful. The 'non-dom' plutocrat, moving to wherever the tax regime is most friendly, certainly exists, but there are far fewer of them than is commonly believed. Tax revenue, in other words, doesn't fall because the rich leave, because the rich haven't actually left.

Another common objection to high or relatively high levels of taxation is that they hamper investment and innovation. By taking money away from the wealth creators, the theory goes, you reduce their willingness to take risks, because you reduce their incentive to do so. Once again, however, there's no solid evidence for this notion. In the first place, countries that have relatively high rates of taxation also happen to have thriving companies that *are* meeting their tax obligation in full. Ironically, any economic disadvantage they suffer is not down to the taxes they are paying but to the unlevel playing field created by their tax-avoiding larger competitors (competitors, it should be added, who are usually the first to shout if they sense distortions in the open working of the free market). One of the great frustrations of many bricks-and-mortar businesses (who are major payers of tax and creators of employment) is that they end up being at a massive disadvantage in comparison to giant online enterprises (who tend to be major tax avoiders and who create far fewer jobs relative to turnover).

Moreover, there are no indications that national success is determined by rates of tax. A study by the IMF of international tax regimes between 1989 and 2011 revealed some, like Japan, which had had low taxation and low growth; and others, like Sweden, which had high taxation and high growth. No correlation at all emerged between rates of taxation and levels of growth.

There are, of course, some highly successful countries that have traditionally adopted low rates of tax. But then there are also very successful ones that have done the opposite. Denmark is a case in point. The average Dane pays about 45 per cent income tax; corporate income tax is 22 per cent and VAT is 25 per cent. Yet not only does Denmark invariably figure at the top of the world's happiest countries, it is also a thriving hub of business, home to such large and well-known companies as Carlsberg, Arla Foods (which makes Lurpak butter), the shipping company Maersk, Lego, Bang & Olufsen and many others. It just goes to show that high tax isn't a barrier to a nation's economic success. The Danish experience seems to bear out the view that legendary investor Warren Buffett expressed in 2011: 'I have worked with investors for sixty years,' he said, 'and I have yet to see anyone ... shy away from a sensible investment because of the tax rate.'

I can only assume that it's because many business leaders have it fixed in their minds that taxation is somehow bad for business (let alone themselves) that they not only fight to have it reduced but believe it's perfectly legitimate to aggressively avoid it. In Britain – which in my view does not operate a particularly high-tax regime – the annual 'tax gap' (that is, the difference between what the Exchequer receives in tax revenue and what it ought to receive as calculated by HMRC) is officially estimated to be in the region of £34 billion. Some campaigners reckon that the true figure is actually much higher, perhaps £120 billion or more (a figure that also tries to take account of the 'unknown unknown' that is missing tax, in other words tax that should be paid but that HMRC has no knowledge of). To put these figures in some sort of context: the recent cuts to living allowances for disabled people, which have caused a lot of hardship, intended to save the government £4 billion a year. The HMRC estimated tax gap is over eight times that figure. The £120 billion gap calculated by some campaigners represents well over twenty-five times the money spent by the government on prisons each year. Richard Brooks' brilliant book *The Great Tax Robbery* is a fascinating – and shocking – account of the various ruses that people use.

Aggressive tax avoidance seems to have become a mini industry in its own right. All sorts of advisers and institutions are on hand to help people create 'offshore' businesses that will enable them to reroute their company's finances through a low-tax haven like Ireland, Luxembourg, or the Cayman Islands, or to park their personal wealth out of sight and reach of the taxman (as the leaked 'Panama Papers' revealed so shockingly in 2015). Labour MP Margaret Hodge's first-class book *Called to Account* offers an eye-opening description of the lengths to which some companies will go to minimise their tax liabilities. An in-depth account of the work of the Parliamentary Public Accounts Committee, which she chaired from 2010 to 2015, it explores the perfectly legal but ethically dubious way in which multinationals such as Google, Starbucks and Amazon managed to pay almost no tax in the UK because, according to their accounts, they made virtually no profits here. Some of the tactics employed involved dizzying levels of accounting sophistry. The 'Dutch sandwich' was and remains one such. Using this method, a company operating in the low-tax culture of the Republic of Ireland can route its money via the Netherlands (taking advantage of the generous tax laws there) to the offshore tax haven of Bermuda. Virtually no tax is paid as the cash moves seamlessly from one jurisdiction to another.

And if such arrangements sound so complicated that only a handful of people are in a position to make use of them, the opposite seems to be the case. In 2015 the BBC broadcast a documentary, *The Town that Took on the Taxman*, that followed the fortunes of a group of local traders in the small Welsh town of Crickhowell as they joined forces to copy the complicated tax arrangements of big business. They found it alarmingly easy to do so. Advisers in tax havens such as the Isle of Man and the Netherlands fell over themselves to help take Crickhowell 'offshore' and, in the process, revealed just how many dodges there are out there. In Amsterdam, for example, it emerged that there were 15,000 'mailbox' companies that existed purely for tax reasons and that allowed eight trillion euros a year to flow in and out of the country, tax free. One of the Dutch accountants who helped the Crickhowell traders set up their own sham company argued there was nothing wrong with this. 'Taxes in my opinion are a choice, the individual choice of every citizen,' he said. It was an interesting interpretation of what others would regard as a civic obligation.

Some legal loopholes exist closer to home. I myself was guilty of exploiting one such over thirty years ago, when I briefly joined a scheme to avoid national insurance that involved paying myself in bullion. A growing sense that this might be above board but not morally justifiable caused me to pull out. Inheritance tax, too, offers the already very wealthy a means of minimising their tax liabilities. According to the current legal framework, which was set up in the 1950s, the rich can put their assets into trusts (which means that they don't 'own' those assets) and so avoid a burden that most others simply have to accept. It was a trust structure that allowed an estate worth £9 billion to pass effortlessly from the 6th Duke of Westminster, who died in 2016, to his son. In the case of the dukes of Westminster the estate in question really is an estate, since the various trusts they hold occupy virtually all the top squares on the Monopoly board: the Duke of Westminster's Grosvenor Estate owns most of Mayfair and Belgravia; the Cadogan Estate, Chelsea and Knightsbridge; the Howard de Walden Estate covers Harley Street and Marylebone; and the Portman Estate includes Oxford Street. Between them, these estates own about £23.8 billion of property in London – all untouched by inheritance tax.

If this seems a very unequal way to organise a country's finances, that's because it is. Most individuals and businesses pay their taxes. But the wealthier you are, the easier it becomes to reduce your tax liability. HMRC appears to accept this state of affairs, or at least be resigned to it, because the way they deal with many of the big players is to negotiate with them rather than to dictate to them. In the course of *The Town that Took on the Taxman*, the Crickhowell traders met Jim Harra, the then-Director General for Business Tax, who revealed that the 2,000 or so largest companies in the UK are treated differently from others in order to 'manage the risk' – in other words HMRC agrees a sum to be paid in return for the company involved not disappearing offshore. As he explained: 'The multinationals are, from our point of view, a high value but also a high risk group and our approach is to man-mark them. So we put a lot of resource into understanding what they're doing.' What this meant back in 2010 for a company such as Vodafone (then the second largest company listed on the UK stock exchange) was a deal whereby decades' worth of tax and interest was reduced from perhaps £7 billion under UK law to £1.25 billion, based on a generous interpretation of EU law. The basis on which this deal was struck remains a secret. As an HMRC spokesman said, 'Our legal obligation to maintain customer confidentiality means we are unable to offer comment on the tax affairs of named individuals or organisations.'

To mend a system that is so clearly broken ultimately requires a degree of international cooperation that is currently sadly lacking. Countries such as Luxembourg will happily continue to negotiate deals with large companies that involve the granting of a favourable rate of corporation tax (usually a fraction of the country's official 29 per cent rate). Countries such as Bermuda will continue to offer zero corporate tax rates and zero personal tax rates. Arguably, Britain could take action against those tax havens over which it has some degree of control (such as the Cayman Islands and the Channel Islands), but it's hard to see how any country would agree to do so unilaterally when there are so many other tax havens that the wealthy can choose from.

But I still think there are practical and constructive steps that could be adopted. First of all, more action needs to be taken to eliminate illegal tax evasion – an area where, in fairness, HMRC has enjoyed some success in recent years. Aggressive tax avoidance could also be policed better. After all, in 2016 and 2017 HMRC won more than twenty tax avoidance cases, suggesting to my mind that there's more that could be clawed back.

Obviously, to do this, the tax authorities need to be given sharper teeth and more resources, and this in turn means an end to government short-termism. One of the stranger paradoxes of recent times has been successive governments' willingness to attack tax evasion while simultaneously cutting back on the people best placed to tackle it. In their book *Dismembered*, Polly Toynbee and David Walker report that under the last administration, HMRC was ordered to cut staff by 5,000 a year (in fact such chaos and poor service ensued that within a year of 5,600 people being made redundant 2,400 had to be re-employed). I am wholly persuaded by the argument put forward in 2013 by the tax managers' union in their 'invest to save' proposal that a £312 million investment in staff (including employing more officials to tackle aggressive tax avoidance by large employers) could bring in more than £8 billion extra in tax over four years. As it is, HMRC has budget cuts scheduled up to 2020. It's the worst type of short-sighted, short-term thinking.

But ultimately, I suspect that the best way to get people and organisations to pay the tax they can so easily afford to pay is to name and shame the guilty parties. I mentioned in Chapter 4 that some Scandinavian countries (Norway, Sweden and Finland) have for many years made publicly available the income tax returns of every taxpayer (Norway now actually posts them online). If Britain followed suit, I suspect there would be a mad scramble among the wealthy – especially celebrities, who care so much about their public image – to make themselves squeaky clean. Anyone who had put their money into clever, entirely legal but ethically dodgy schemes would be rushing to take it out again. One only needs to think of the embarrassment caused to various high-profile names by the leak of the 'Paradise Papers' in 2017 to appreciate just how powerful openness can be.

By the same token, I believe that the workings of HMRC should be equally transparent. It's shocking to think that the Vodafone tax deal I mentioned earlier only came to light because a whistle-blower was prepared to stick their head above the parapet. I would shine a light, too, on those accountancy firms – notably Britain's 'Big Four' – who make so much money out of the aggressive tax avoidance schemes they concoct, regardless of whether those schemes are later disallowed. The fact that some of these companies are profiting from public sector contracts while simultaneously helping clients to avoid what I regard as a public duty is particularly galling.

For businesses, as I have said before, reputation is everything. And Britain doesn't like tax avoiders. In a 2017 poll commissioned by Christian Aid nearly nine out of ten of the British adults surveyed expressed the view that tax avoidance by large companies is morally wrong even if it is legal. The study also found that 85 per cent thought that it is too easy for large companies in the UK to avoid paying tax, and that one in four people were already boycotting the products or services of a company because they felt it did not pay its fair share of tax. That is a large number of people taking action against perceived tax avoiders. If the public had a clearer idea of who all those avoiders are, they could do some real damage to the parties involved.

Tax law is complicated, but the basic principle is simple. Everyone who lives, works or owns a business in this country gets something out of our society. It therefore follows that everyone who lives, works or owns a business here needs to pay their share back into the nation's coffers at a rate that is proportional to their income. This is an idea that most people understand perfectly well, but that some big companies and rich individuals don't seem to get. It's a view that has to change.

CHAPTER 6

THE LIMITS OF CAPITALISM

THE STATE AND PRIVATE ENTERPRISE

IF THE 1970S marked the moment when the idea of shareholder value gained traction, it was also the period – particularly in Britain – when 'big government' began to be questioned and the case was made ever more strongly for the involvement of private enterprise in public services and state-run industries. Given the nature of the times, this was hardly surprising. With its economic slow-down, oil crisis, high inflation and high unemployment, it was a pretty grim decade. Britain was hit by constant strikes, there was intransigence among both bosses and unions, and public services declined. Ultimately the Labour government of Jim Callaghan had to suffer the humiliation of approaching the IMF for a loan. Things clearly weren't working.

It's now sometimes forgotten that the reason why particular enterprises were taken into state ownership was that under private management they had either not been offering the level of service people wanted or had been struggling financially. The car manufacturer British Leyland, which was partly nationalised in 1975, is a case in point. But arguably it's precisely companies such as British Leyland that demonstrated to critics of nationalisation all the faults of public ownership. As a largely state-owned business, British Leyland suffered from poor industrial relations and poor productivity, and it produced cars that were often poor quality. Germany boasted such companies as BMW and Mercedes-Benz. Britain, nationalisation critics would have argued, had the Morris Marina. And if you wanted the ultimate case against state involvement in car manufacturing you had only to look to Eastern Europe and its Ladas and Trabants. For those who wanted indifferent products shoddily finished, it seemed, the state sector was the answer. For those who wanted efficiency, value for money, and constant innovation and improvement, the private sector was the place to be.

Today, when it comes to balancing what the state manages and what private enterprise controls, there's quite a divergence of approach among countries that could be broadly categorised as capitalist. France has a long tradition of state intervention in business stretching back to the seventeenth century, though this has constantly been adjusted and rebalanced. The US tends to be wary of strong control from the centre (and, of course, doesn't have a national health service). Britain has moved from relatively high levels of state supervision in the decades after the Second World War to an approach now that makes greater use of private enterprise in areas such as utilities and infrastructure. No two countries draw the line in quite the same place, though all accept that just as there are areas which the state alone can and should run, there are some things much better left to the private sector.

So where should the line be drawn? Does state involvement generally spell problems with efficiency and value for money? Is it always the case that where free enterprise can be given a role it will manage things better, more smartly and more innovatively? In other words, if you involve private businesses as much as possible in delivering public services, do you always get a BMW rather than a Trabant?

An area where it's actually possible to test this hypothesis is, on the surface at least, a rather surprising one: prisons.

In earlier times, British prisons were small-scale operations that for the most part were funded locally. This changed in the nineteenth century as imprisonment became an ever more common form of punishment and the costs of administering and running prisons rose accordingly. Central government increasingly stepped in to build and maintain a national network of jails. There was an intellectual as well as a practical justification for this. If the administration of justice was a fundamental concern of central government, it was felt, then it made sense for the administration of punishment to be under government control as well.

In recent years, however, a private element has been introduced to the running of Britain's prisons. This has been partly ideologically driven, promoted both by those who favour privatisation in general and by those in political circles who know that the niceties of the prison system are not vote winners. It has partly been promoted by private enterprise spotting an opportunity. But it's also been a practical response to a problem. Quite simply, we're locking up more people than ever before. The prison population has doubled since 1980, and there are now more than 85,000 inmates (Britain has one of the highest incarceration rates in Europe). What's more, we're not keeping pace with demand. In the past thirty years, the Prison Reform Trust reports, an extra 32,000 prison places have been added, but an additional 40,000 people have been imprisoned. The majority are serving short sentences, for non-violent crimes, but the fact remains that the system cannot cope. Hence the reason for turning to the private sector.

Privately run prisons were first introduced in the 1990s and there are currently fourteen of them in England and Wales. The contracts are in the hands of three companies, Serco, G4S and Sodexo, all of which also hold many other public service contracts. In some cases the private contractors have been brought in to take over the running of existing prisons. In others, private contractors have both built and then run new prisons.

The result has been a disaster in quite a few cases. There has been some appalling mismanagement, and there has also been financial scandal: in 2013 G4S and Serco were found to have wrongly overcharged the Ministry of Justice by several million pounds for tagging people who did not require monitoring (in some cases, the people involved were no longer living). Just how bad things could be was exposed by a BBC *Panorama* programme in 2017 which examined the horrendous situation at HMP Northumberland, 'managed' by Sodexo Justice Services, where the most hardened of the inmates appeared to have more control than the staff. 'It didn't take too long to realise that the inmates were, in effect, running this prison,' said *Panorama* reporter Joe Fenton, who filmed while working undercover as a prison officer. 'I saw prisoners stumbling around drunk, others who were high on drugs … On a standard ten-hour shift, the demands from prisoners were endless.' Staff struggled to cope, he said. Drugs – notably the strong synthetic drug 'spice' – were being smuggled in. At least three members of staff, *Panorama* was told, had required hospital treatment after accidentally inhaling spice smoke. 'Our vision is to develop it into a working prison, providing meaningful work for prisoners which will lead to enhanced employment opportunities on their release,' Sodexo had stated in 2013. 'Prisoners are in prison for a reason and prisons must exist to both punish and rehabilitate. But from my experience, I didn't see much of either,' Fenton concluded.

Panorama's findings were confirmed by HM Inspectorate of Prisons later in 2017. The inspectors found that violence at Northumberland had more than doubled since its last inspection in 2014, with 58 per cent of prisoners saying that they had felt unsafe at some time – a significantly higher percentage than that recorded in comparable prisons. As for the drug problem: 21 per cent of prisoners told inspectors that they had acquired a drug habit *since* entering the prison.

I'm not pretending that there aren't plenty of problems in publicly run prisons. Britain's prison system overall is antiquated and creaking: many inmates are housed in decaying Victorian buildings that are wholly inadequate for a twenty-first-century prison system. They, too, face daily problems with violence and drug abuse. As HM Chief Inspector of Prisons said in his 2016–17 annual report: 'I have been appalled by the conditions in which we hold many prisoners. Far too often I have seen men sharing a cell in which they are locked up for as much as 23 hours a day, in which they are required to eat all their meals and in which there is an unscreened lavatory.' But the fact that there are private prisons that are no better – indeed, arguably, worse – surely brings into stark question whether private is always best.

It is bad enough in my view that Britain has never really worked out what it thinks its prisons are for. Are they there simply to take offenders off the street and to punish them? Are they supposed to deter bad people from future wrongdoing? Are they supposed to reassure the public that justice is being served? And if – as is presumably the case – the answer is a mixture of all three, how does that square with our simultaneous hope that prisoners will somehow learn to reform their ways in jail, be rehabilitated, and so never offend again? (In fact 49 per cent of adults are reconvicted within a year of leaving jail – a truly shocking indictment of our prison system.)

But if to that hopeless muddle of aims, you add yet a further, irreconcilable one – to make a profit – you make a bad situation far worse. The contract for HMP Northumberland is a depressing example. It's worth £250 million over its fifteen-year term, and supposedly represents savings for the government of £129.8 million over its lifetime. The assumption at the time, presumably, was that through the wonders of private enterprise Sodexo would both run a prison well and make a profit.

But this is where the contract system goes disastrously wrong, because in most public services there is only one way to make significant savings, and that is by reducing the workforce. HMP Northumberland had 270 frontline staff when Sodexo took over (a figure that was already down on the 440 it had a few years previously). The company reduced this to 192 staff, for 1,300 inmates. It proved a risky strategy. An understaffed prison rapidly goes into a spiral of decline. Because there are not enough officers to supervise activities, prisoners are locked in their cells for most of the day. That makes them even more angry and desperate – more suicidal, more drug-dependent, and more violent.

A similar shambles has taken place at Yarl's Wood Immigration Removal Centre in Bedfordshire, managed by Serco. Here again, it's never been clear how overall policy, budget and level of care were meant to align, and a debacle has inevitably followed. A series of scandals over recent years have revealed a failure to consider who should be sent there in the first place (many of the predominantly female inmates have committed no crime, some are the survivors of sexual violence who shouldn't be there at all, some have been locked up indefinitely); a failure of care once they are there (conditions are harsh; levels of depression are worryingly high, and there were 64 attempted suicides in 2015 alone); 'insufficient operational and management staff', according to the National Audit Office in 2016 (as with Sodexo, Serco have cut back on numbers); and some truly bizarre and cruel practices that have resulted from Home Office performance targets (a £10,000 penalty for each escape led Serco to handcuff women on hospital visits). Serco's contract to run the detention centre was renewed for a further eight years in 2014 at a cost of £70 million.

Successful private businesses have a clear sense of what they want to do and how they are going to achieve it. If that clarity is not there, the outcome is rarely a positive one. In a classic free market situation, there will be a readily identifiable customer, a good product or service that is designed to appeal to them, and competition from others to ensure honesty, value for money and improvements over time to the goods or service. With private prisons, it's not apparent who the 'customer' is (is it the prisoners or Her Majesty's Prison and Probation Service – or in the case of Yarl's Wood, the Home

Office?). Competition is effectively limited to three very similar companies who can prove contractually difficult to displace if things go wrong. In the midst of all this, what should be the goal of the enterprise – to ensure that prisoners (or detainees) are safe and to offer them a chance for rehabilitation – is lost.

The profit element distorts things further, since it's derived from a very narrow interpretation of what constitutes value for money. If by using a private prison the costs of incarcerating a prisoner can be reduced and that prisoner is then rehabilitated and doesn't reoffend, the savings are genuine savings. But we know that poor prison conditions increase the chances of reoffending and that, according to the National Audit Office, reoffending in England and Wales costs the taxpayer up to £10 billion a year in terms of police and court time, NHS and social care expenditure, and so on. Then there's the social and psychological impact of re-offending on individuals and communities. Not to make an allowance for all that in the calculation of expenditure and savings is highly misleading.

Prisons represent a huge challenge to society. They house some of its most vulnerable members (in his history of violence in England, Professor James Sharpe points out that a government White Paper in 2002 calculated that people in prison 'are thirteen times more likely to have been in care as a child, ten times more likely to have been a regular truant from school, thirteen times more likely to be unemployed, two and a half times more likely to have a close relative with a criminal conviction, and six times more likely to have been a young parent'). Yet one cannot ignore the fact that these are also people who have committed crimes that have damaged others' lives. They need to be punished but they also need help. In all this, they're unlikely to command much sympathy or support from the wider community or from politicians. One thing is for certain, though: dealing with the problem that prisons pose through a cost-effective, profit-driven formula is never going to be the answer, unless relevant key performance indicators are very carefully factored into the tendering process and are then closely monitored.

The failure of private prisons, to my mind, shows just how difficult, if not impossible, it is to apply the principles of the free market in every part of our lives. Capitalism works best when it involves fairly straightforward transactions in a market that is as open and competitive as possible. Running a prison fulfils none of those criteria.

Even when the transaction involved is quite straightforward, a capitalist approach will not work well if the other conditions are not met. That 'open and competitive' element I've just mentioned is absolutely crucial. Without it, there are no – or, at least, insufficient – pressures on an enterprise to offer the best goods or services it can. It will become complacent. It will inevitably focus on profit and cut corners to achieve that profit. In an open market, there are external pressures to balance profit vs service vs investment, and so on. In a closed, monopolistic market there are none. It comes as no surprise that canny US investor Warren Buffet is so keen on what he calls 'toll booths' – companies that have total control of a particular sector.

The nation's water supply is the obvious example here. Whether it's in state hands (as in Britain it once was) or in private ones, it can, for obvious reasons, only be obtained from a single, regional provider. There is, essentially, no competition. True, a private provider could lose their operating licence if they offered a consistently bad service, but that doesn't mask the fact that on a day-to-day basis it is impossible to make the sector competitive. If you live in York, you have to use Yorkshire Water.

When the water industry was privatised in 1989, the justification offered was that it needed major new investment. Pipes and sewage systems, many of which dated back to Victorian times, were in terrible condition. Urgent upgrades were required.

Nearly thirty years later, and it's questionable whether things have significantly improved. Concerns about infrastructure and service constantly arise. Planning for periods of low rainfall has frequently proved inadequate. The system leaks (according to the regulator Ofwat, a quarter of the water pumped in London fails to reach customers). Burst pipes are a constant problem (20,000 homes in the capital were left without water for several days following the cold snap of March 2018). There are periodic problems with pollution (in 2017 Thames Water was fined £20 million for repeatedly discharging untreated or poorly treated sewage into the Thames and its tributaries). Thames Water's defence tends to be that it's having to cope with an antiquated pipe and sewage system (38 per cent of the network was built before 1930). Whether that's an excuse that can be justified nearly thirty years after privatisation is dubious. If the system was still in public hands, it's certainly not an excuse that would be accepted by advocates of privatisation.

If it's questionable whether privatisation has brought customers a better service, it's also highly dubious whether it's resulted in better value for money. The precise financial workings of the water industry are somewhat shadowy, since six of the nine companies that serve England are not listed on the stock market and so don't have to release information to shareholders that others can then see. But it appears that profits have in no small part arisen simply from piling on debt. In an outraged article in the *Spectator*, Nick Cohen noted: 'Researchers at Greenwich University say that in the past decade, the nine companies have made £18.8 billion of post-tax profits. Far from using the money to make the water system better, they have paid out £18.1 billion in dividends, and financed investment through loading £42 billion of debt on to consumers.' Needless to say, senior executives are breathtakingly well rewarded. If ever proof of the dangers of private monopolies was needed, this is it.

It doesn't help that water is a monopoly whose ownership is so often at arm's-length. Northumbrian Water is owned by Cheung Kong Infrastructure Holdings in Hong Kong. Wessex Water is owned by the Malaysian YTL Corporation. Thames Water was owned by a consortium led by the Australian Macquarie Group (who left it with an extra £2 billion of debt) which sold its final stake to the Canadian pension fund OMERS and the Kuwait Investment Authority. This is not a great recipe for local accountability.

Problems can also arise in sectors where a monopoly situation is not quite as clear-cut. With gas and electricity, consumers are at least in a position to switch suppliers if they're unhappy with the

service they're receiving, and that theoretically intro-
duces a degree of competition into the market. But
this small element of choice still doesn't create an
openly competitive market in the normally under-
stood form of the term. Because the services these
companies offer are so vital, you can't let a badly
run company simply collapse. And you can't leave
all the vast costs involved in supplying power and
energy to individual companies to handle because
they'll either end up having to pass them on to the
consumer, which will make their goods and services
unaffordable, or they themselves will have to absorb
the costs, which will make them unprofitable. In
this context, it's worth bearing in mind that the cost
just of decommissioning Britain's old nuclear power
stations will be huge and spread over many years.
Clearing up Sellafield, Calder Hill and Windscale
alone could involve a £117 billion bill, according to
official estimates.

The country's built infrastructure – in the form of
roads, railways, bridges and so on – poses similar
challenges. Here, historically, the cost of construction
and maintenance has proved to be so great relative
to the revenue that a particular project can generate
that private enterprise has rarely proved a practical
solution in the long term. Attempts to overhaul
Britain's roads in the eighteenth and nineteenth

centuries via 30,000 miles or so of privately funded toll roads gave way, in the face of competition from the railways, to state control. The privately funded railways in their turn started to struggle once cars became popular (something privatisation apologists tend to forget), and, again, the state intervened.

Champions of private enterprise would no doubt point to the Channel Tunnel as an example of a successful, highly ambitious, privately funded engineering project. Leaving aside, however, the fact that, like so many public projects, it ran massively over budget and had to reschedule its debts, it took twenty-six years to turn its first real profit. It's a triumphant piece of engineering. It's not a financial model for future grand projects.

Because so much of the funding for infrastructure comes from central government, it's very difficult indeed to judge whether such private involvement as there has been in, for example, the running of the railways has been as beneficial as free marketeers have claimed or as damaging as fans of state control have argued. As with a utility company, so an enterprise such as a regional rail operator is dealing with only part of the overall railway equation. Running an audit that measures value for money and service in a sector of such complexity is not easy.

That said, events over the past decade or so suggest to me that the case for private involvement is far from proven. East Coast rail offers an interesting case study in this respect. In 2009 its operating company, National Express, experienced major financial problems and the franchise collapsed. The service therefore had to be rescued by a government controlled company which proceeded to run it for six years until 2015, when the franchise was returned to the private sector. In those six years, passenger satisfaction rates rose to 91 per cent, and in its final twelve months in operation, the government controlled company saw ticket sales rise, and was able to hand back £208.7 million to Department for Transport coffers. Compare that with the ongoing woes at private operator Southern Rail, with its constant cancellations, overcrowded trains and terrible industrial relations – or indeed with the recent debacle on the reprivatised East Coast routes which has resulted in an announcement that the operating company, Stagecoach, will terminate its franchise early because, as the Transport Secretary put it, it 'got its numbers wrong'. Public ownership does not automatically involve bad management; private control does not necessarily mean good management.

The other area where I believe the free market does not operate well is the one which, for want of a better term, I would call the social sector: the schools, hospitals, housing and other basic building blocks of a society that are essential to all. Since these are not natural monopolies, it's perfectly possible, of course, to have private and publicly funded enterprises side by side (though, arguably, part of the reason why public services are often so poor is that the people with money and influence don't have to use them). It's nevertheless noteworthy how small a proportion of the overall responsibility for each sector private enterprise is able to support. Private education accounts for the education of no more than 7 per cent of schoolchildren in the UK at any given time. Only around 4 million people have private health insurance (and most of these will in any case use a mixture of public and private healthcare systems). More people own their own homes than don't (64 per cent as of 2016), but the overall figure involved has dropped and is continuing to fall as Britain's housing stock has become ever more unaffordable for first-time buyers.

Everybody needs and deserves an education, healthcare and somewhere to live. Only a tiny minority could afford these if all three were simply left to the open market. Heavy state involvement is therefore essential. And what experience has shown is that when the state then attempts to pass or delegate responsibility for the majority to a free market that would otherwise trade only with a minority, the outcome is rarely a positive one.

The current social housing crisis offers perhaps the starkest instance of this. It's a crisis that has its roots in policy decisions taken in the 1980s. Up until then there had been a fairly sustained programme of provision, kick-started by Prime Minister Lloyd George's determination at the end of the First World War to create 'Homes fit for Heroes', and the law passed in 1919 that required local authorities to provide council housing wherever needed. Not all the council housing built was of good quality – particularly during the 1960s and 1970s rush to replace old slum housing as cheaply and quickly as possible – but it was at least being created.

In the 1980s, however, there was a change of policy. Previously, council houses had passed from individual to individual or family to family as required. Now the current tenant was offered the wherewithal to buy the property in which they lived at a discount. Between 1980 and 2013 some 1.87 million council homes passed into private ownership.

In itself the understandably popular 'right to buy' scheme did not create the problems we face today, even though it did often involve the selling off of council assets at below their market value or replacement cost. However, in addition to forcing local authorities to dispose of their properties to those prepared to buy them, the government also placed restrictions on what they could and couldn't do with the proceeds. Quite simply, councils found themselves selling off housing stock and not being allowed to invest in replacing it.

Theoretically, of course, this is where the private sector was meant to step in. And indeed in the decade between 2003 and 2014 the number of privately rented homes in England and Wales increased from 2.5 million to nearly 4.6 million. The law of supply and demand, it seems, has been fully at work and could be seen to be working.

But there are two problems with this rosy view of the tidy workings of the free market. The first is that because the number of families and people living on their own has increased sharply in recent years, demand has outstripped supply and so pushed up prices. The second is that those prices can, for the most part, only be afforded by those fortunate enough to be in a good, steady job. For the unemployed, or those suffering from a chronic illness or disability, the private option has now effectively been taken out of their reach. For those not in regular employment – including workers on zero-hours contracts – the lack of a guaranteed income means that private landlords will not rent to them.

At present there are 1.16 million households on lists maintained by local authorities who are either waiting for a council property or one managed by a housing association. If they're fortunate enough to be offered a place to live they'll pay on average £87.20 in weekly rent for a secure council tenancy and £96.61 for housing association accommodation. If they have to turn to the private sector they will pay twice to three times as much. That 1.16 million figure, however, is only part of the equation, and ignores the many others who, for whatever reason, are unable to get on the housing list. According to Shelter chief executive Polly Neate, hundreds of thousands of others are 'Hidden away in emergency B&B's, temporary bedsits and on friends' sofas', of whom perhaps 128,000 are children. A growing number have literally nowhere to go and end up on the streets. It's been estimated that in 2017 an estimated 4,751 people each night bedded down on pavements and in shop doorways – a 15 per cent increase on the previous year and a 169 per cent increase since 2010.

As with prisons, so with housing. A highly complex social need has been reduced to a simplistic and distorted market equation, the inevitable result of which has been disastrous. Private landlords meet some of the need for accommodation among the worst off and most vulnerable, but only because they are effectively subsidized by housing benefits to the tune of £9 billion a year (money which then helps inflate and distort property prices across the private and social sector alike). Housing associations, part state-funded, part free-market operators, build comparatively little and some pay their chief executives vast salaries. Councils have responsibility (in 2016 they spent an estimated £845 million on temporary accommodation), but they also have little real power to increase the housing supply.

And in the midst of all this people are suffering terribly. Conditions in B&Bs have frequently been found to be unsafe and unsanitary. Those forced to live in such places are prone to physical and mental health problems, and their chances of employment are greatly reduced. A grim National Audit Office report in 2017 described the 'further unquantified cost of homelessness to wider public services', highlighting 'the additional burden on public services of homeless people who experience poorer health outcomes, or require more public sector intervention than the average person. It includes admissions to hospital and outpatient services, policing, and costs to the justice system.'

So far I have focused on where and why the private sector is not always the answer. But then the public ownership and supervision that often preceded it was scarcely problem-free either. Private companies have been guilty of poor service, incompetence and greed.

Publicly run enterprises have been guilty of poor service, incompetence and bureaucratic overload. Is there really much to choose between them? To answer that, I think one first needs to consider ownership and management separately.

To my mind the intellectual case for public ownership of key public utilities and services is an overwhelming one. As I hope I've demonstrated, the private sector simply doesn't have the deep pockets needed to support an entire nuclear programme, say, or to maintain the nation's roads and bridges. Railtrack, for example, which was given responsibility for the country's rail infrastructure, had to be replaced by the government-owned Network Rail in the aftermath of the Hatfield rail disaster of 2000. Metronet, a public-private partnership with London Underground responsible for the maintenance and upgrade of nine Tube lines, went into administration in 2007 and its responsibilities were handed back to public ownership in 2008. The National Audit Office later calculated that the failure of Metronet's contract had cost the taxpayer over £400 million.

Where the assets on offer have been more attractive, the law of unintended consequences has invariably come into play. The right to buy scheme, for instance, may have helped many former council tenants as originally intended, but it also enriched buy-to-let landlords, who by 2015, according to an

Inside Housing study, were in possession of nearly four in ten ex-council houses.

When it comes to creating new infrastructure, the public sector tends again to be the far better bet. Governments can borrow more cheaply than the private sector because government-backed gilts are lower risk. Where local authorities are seeking to build on their own land, it makes similar sense for them to retain ownership. The low cost of borrowing means that ultimately it will be much cheaper for them to build and then house people than to farm tenants out to the private rental sector.

The wholly disastrous private finance initiative (PFI) has unfortunately masked just how financially efficient central and local government ownership can be. Invented by a Conservative government in 1992 and then popularised by a Labour administration after 1997, it was designed to get big projects such as new hospitals and schools off the ground by handing over the work to private companies and leasing back the end product over a period of years. According to the National Audit Office, 700 PFI contracts worth a total of £60 billion have so far been issued.

But as I've said before, you get nowt for nowt. In reality, the system of tender by which private builders and developers have been brought on board has been deeply flawed. The government has signed contracts over which it has little subsequent control and which commit it to repayments at extortionate interest rates over twenty-five to thirty years. And the private contractors do what private contractors do: they seek to maximise their profits (one proposed deal for military dog kennels would have ended up costing more per night per dog than a room in London's Park Lane Hilton); or, as with Carillion, they fail to balance their books and go bust. Private investors in PFI (of whom I admit I was one, many years ago) have generally done very nicely out of the financial sleight of hand that PFI represents (many deals regularly offer a 20 per cent return). Meanwhile, the tax payer will be left to pick up the tab – some £199 billion in charges over the next twenty-five years according to the National Audit Office. That in practice successive governments have been danger-ously short-sighted does not, however, mean that the principle of public ownership doesn't work.

When it comes to running, as opposed to owning, a concern, there has long been the view that this is something that the private sector does much better. Its focus on profit makes it efficient and lean. Public bodies tend to be bloated and incompetent.

Experience, though, suggests that good and bad management crop up everywhere. It's not the nature of an organisation's ownership that deter-mines the quality of its leadership, in my view;

it's the nature of its goals and the quality of its people and how they're managed. A privately run bank focused purely on profit will acquire leaders who cut corners to achieve that profit. A state-run car manufacturer focused purely on day-to-day survival will acquire leaders who compromise on investment to try to ensure that survival.

And when goals are muddled or messy compromises, as so often happens with the social sector, the way in which an organisation is run is even more compromised. The recent history of the Royal Mail demonstrates the problem. When it was in public hands it had to cope with a wildly contradictory set of business objectives. It had to offer universal delivery in the declining and ever less profitable letters part of its remit. But its powers to fund this by the obvious mechanism of raising the price of first- and second-class mail were severely circumscribed by central government. And since it had been forced to open up its very lucrative parcels sector to competition, it couldn't simply use one part of the business to subsidise the other. Once the government made the decision to sell the business off, the rules changed. The price of a first-class stamp was allowed to rise immediately and steeply from 46p to 60p and then from 60p to 65p; fierce cost-cutting was then allowed when the service was sold off. The issue here is not whether privatising Royal

Mail was the right thing to do (cases can be made on both sides, though there's no doubt that because the government set a low share price, the taxpayer lost out to the tune of between £180 million – according to one official report – and £1 billion – according to a Commons select committee). The issue is that, when in public ownership, the goals Royal Mail was set were confused ones.

And here, I think, we reach the nub of the problems that are so often associated with the public sector. When there's a clear sense of what has to be done, and the organisation involved is then left to get on with it, the result is generally a positive one: having crashed in the financial crisis of 2007–8, Lloyds was effectively nationalised for several years, returned to a sound footing, and then sold off again. But central government projects have an unfortunate tendency to be political footballs. Time and time again, the goalposts are moved, short-term expedients are urged, and impossible circles are expected to be squared. The more cynical have suggested an ulterior motive here: setting up the public sector to fail in particular areas opens the door to privatisation. Be that as it may, it's unquestionably the case that no organisation can thrive in that kind of environment.

The effective CEOs of these public organisations – government ministers – don't help. Appointed on a whim, often regardless of previous knowledge or expertise, prone or forced to make snap decisions, and then moved on swiftly to another job, they are ill placed to offer either thoughtful policy-making or continuity. It's hard to think of the shambles of the prison system without also noting that between 2015 and 2018 five people have served as Secretary of State for Justice. It's likewise difficult to reconcile the coherent approach to education that every country needs with the musical chairs that have been played at the Department for Education in recent years. If a publicly listed company changed its CEO that often, its shareholders would be right to be deeply concerned.

When, therefore, big public projects are mishandled – as they are on a regular basis – you have to ask to what extent this is simply the inevitable consequence of leaving execution to government departments and to what extent it is the inescapable result of leaving complex initial decisions and subsequent oversight to political appointees. That government departments mess up is unquestionable. You only have to think of the poor way in which many service and PFI contracts have been drafted (did the contract with Sodexo for HMP Northumberland stipulate a minimum ratio of officers to prisoners? Did the PFI contract for the school that was costing Liverpool council £12,000 a day two years after the school closed consider this eventuality?). Then there are the mismanaged projects, such as the National Programme for IT in the NHS, which was supposed to hold all patient records and would have been the world's largest civilian computer system, but was so badly handled that it had to be abandoned, having already cost the taxpayer nearly £10 billion. Other examples abound.

I also suspect that the relationship between civil servants in procurement departments and the businesses with whom they deal is sometimes a little too cosy and insufficiently transparent. In 2016 it emerged that over the previous few years dozens of senior officials and military staff at the Ministry of Defence had left to take jobs with defence contractors, while a significant number of Treasury staff had moved over to the banking and business world. Many had been allowed to do this without proper vetting, and those whose cases had been considered by the Advisory Committee on Business Appointments (ACOBA), which oversees civil servants and ministers in this area, had invariably been cleared to do so. It's hard not to fear potential conflicts of interest here, particularly as ACOBA rules dictate that only a year has to elapse before a former civil servant or minister can take up a private role. Similar potential conflicts of interest occur in local government, too.

But while I think there are always criticisms that can be levelled at those who administer the country's public infrastructure, it's hard to avoid the suspicion that it's the political element in decision-making that is most corrosive. Contracts may get placed to guarantee jobs in key constituencies or to keep particular interest groups happy. Or they're announced in order to win headlines but before they've been properly costed. Goalposts are constantly moved as political agendas shift – one sure way to ensure that already complex projects spiral out of control.

And if civil servants are open to temptation and undue influence from private suppliers and contractors, so are politicians. They are wined and dined, some excessively, by lobby groups. Special interest groups push for particular policies (it's worth remembering that the rolling programme of privatisation – which has invariably involved setting a low initial share price and whose complexities involve paying big fees – has benefited big city institutions far more than it has helped individual taxpayers). Property developers press those in local government for planning consents. Moreover, politicians can top up their parliamentary salaries by taking on consultancy work. Access to politicians is a valuable commodity. Before David Cameron became Prime Minister, for example, business leaders were offered membership of his Leader's Group which offered access to senior political figures in return for a £50,000 donation to party funds. I'll freely admit that curiosity drove me to join for a while.

I have some sympathy for politicians, who I think have difficult jobs for which they are insufficiently remunerated. But it's not healthy that they can so easily earn money in ways that compromise their independence. It would be far better, I believe, to pay them more and ban them from taking on outside work. That way, at least, we would avoid the spectacle of ex-Labour ministers joining consultancy firms in spheres related to their former briefs, or former Conservative cabinet ministers taking on advisory work for hire.

The party political approach to public services has, sadly, clouded all discussion of how best to organise things in the future. Those on the left have recently argued for a return to the levels of public ownership last seen in the 1970s. Those on the right reject all such calls outright, and continue to argue that private is best.

My own stance is less party political and more pragmatic. I suspect that the renationalisation ship has long sailed – it's simply too expensive to take all key utilities back into public ownership, and I don't believe in any case that every move to involve the private sector has been wrong. In areas where real competition has been possible – telecoms is one such – privatisation has arguably helped bring about lower prices, greater choice and more innovation (though, as I mentioned before, it's worth noting that central government is being expected to help with broadband connections). Water is perhaps the clearest-cut instance of a privatisation too far. To that I would be inclined to add nuclear energy and prisons. So far as other sectors are concerned, I'm open minded: all that ultimately matters is that they are run well and that they are run to serve those who need them.

In highly complex areas like housing, I don't think a one-size-fits-all approach is sufficient. I certainly believe that councils should be free to borrow in order to build social housing – and not the drab estates of the past, but well-designed, environmentally friendly, low-rent homes of the type that are to be found in Scandinavia, Holland and Germany. I also think councils should be allowed and encouraged to leverage the enormous bargaining power that control of planning permission gives them to force developers to build genuinely more affordable housing than they are at present creating. And affordable should mean affordable: the current government rule that affordable means 20 per cent below marketplace prices is hopelessly inadequate.

Where private initiatives have taken hold, they have to be fully accountable. It seems extraordinary to me that the government can allow academy schools to be set up (which are still state schools, despite the name), pour in public funding to them and then allow failing ones (of which there have been quite a few) to strip assets from the schools they were managing and leave taxpayers to foot the final bill. Yet this is what happened in 2017 with Wakefield City Academies Trust, which up until that September had been responsible for twenty-one Yorkshire schools. One of the principles behind academy schools is that they don't have to answer to their local education authority. But they do need to answer to someone.

In other areas, where I believe public sector control is crucial – as, for example, with healthcare – the aim should be less government interference on a day-to-day basis and an ideally less fragmentary approach to management. No corporation would run its operations as the NHS does, with dozens of individual trusts, all hiring separately, buying separately and generally reinventing the wheel all around the country. As Margaret Hodge notes in her book, *Called to Account*, that way we end up with a situation where health trusts buy 652 different types of surgical gloves between them. No doubt a cynic would say that such an expensive muddle is the inevitable consequence of public ownership. It's worth bearing in mind, though, that the US, with its strong emphasis on the private sector, actually spends more per head of population on healthcare than any other country (and yet doesn't top the list of best health services in the world).

Well-run corporations look for economies of scale and best practice that can be rolled out to everyone. The principle of *kaizen* – continuous improvement – which I have found has delivered massive benefits to my own company, demands that we seek out the best way to do something, impose a rule to ensure everyone does it that way, and constantly look for ways to do it better. Continuous improvement is surely vital in services like health, education, social work and the emergency services. Unfortunately, the structure of these services hampers managers' ability to put it into place.

This is all a question of management, not owner-ship. There is no reason why, given top-quality managers (supported by well-paid and, one would hope, well-rewarded staff) and the ability to borrow judiciously to invest, any public service could not do a first-class job. Why not aim for public health-care and education that is so good no one wants to go private? If you take into account all the hidden costs of the current system, from PFI interest payments, to non-taxpaying charitable status for private schools, to government subsidies and top-ups, it would not be as expensive as might at first appear. Certainly we could end up with a much fairer and happier society that way.

But the issues need to be properly explained and honestly discussed, and we all need to be encouraged to join the debate.

CONCLUSION

I'VE ALWAYS LIKED the concept of active luck and passive luck. Active luck is not really luck but something that a person creates themselves by seizing opportunities, taking the initiative and working hard. When people look at a successful person and say, 'Aren't they lucky?' the chances are that that person has a lot of active luck.

Passive luck really is luck, because we don't control it ourselves. I've been able to have a successful and enjoyable career because I had the passive luck of being born in the UK, in a peaceful period of history. I had the health, education and freedom to be able to start my own business and pursue my ambitions. Furthermore, the conditions in society around me meant that there were energetic and capable people who wanted to work for my company, and customers with money in their pockets to buy from us, and state infrastructure in place to make all this possible.

Many people in business or in public life will have had a large helping of passive luck – not all, of course, as some can point to enormous achievements despite starting out in difficult circumstances. All of us benefit from the passive luck of having a stable and civilised society supporting us.

The question is: what are we doing with that luck? Are we using it just to further our own interests or are we using it to help other people thrive?

In this book I've argued that treating people well is good for business, and I believe strongly that the ethical business will be a successful business. I hope that readers will go away wanting to treat their employees, colleagues and customers better, and having a few new ideas for how to do so.

Once success has been achieved, there is so much more that business people can do. Instead of retreating behind their big gates and congratulating themselves on how well they've done, they should be using their skills and influence to do some good in society. They can think about their legacy in much wider terms than simply leaving money for their family (I don't even believe it's a good thing for people to inherit too much).

Society is at a critical juncture. Inequality is running out of control in the UK and, if it continues to widen, will threaten the fabric of society. Those who are rich and secure cannot cut themselves off from other people's misery. We need to create a culture of fairness before the dam bursts.

No business is an island. However much successful people like to think they are self-made, they would be nowhere without the society that surrounds them, and the support, security and economic stability that society provides. They would be nowhere without other people: they need a workforce and customers just as much as that workforce and those customers need them.

So if readers are thinking, 'Fine, but what can I do?' the answer is – a lot. It may not be possible to change the big things, except ultimately, perhaps, through the ballot box. But if even a stereo salesman like me can find ways to get involved in helping people and trying to change things for the better, then hopefully others can, too. And, if you are a business person, this experience can be invaluable if used well. Most entrepreneurs are innovative, persistent and determined, exactly the qualities needed to create change in the world.

What I've done over the years is to pick up on issues which concern me and investigate how my skills, contacts and financial support might help. I've focused on issues where it seemed that not enough was being done. I've looked for ways in which support for a small charity, say, can bring about change that will make a difference.

I had the idea of helping people in poverty through a charity that would link the donor with the person in need via the internet without intermediaries. The Archbishop of York, Dr John Sentamu, took up the challenge and came up with the name Acts 435. We launched it at the General Synod of the Church of England in 2010. I realised that the Church has people on the ground who know their communities and can see the best way to help individuals in need – they had the expertise, what they needed was the money to get started. It's an incredibly efficient charity, with running costs now funded entirely from Gift Aid, so 100 per cent of donations goes towards helping many thousands of people. Its achievements range from supporting a troubled mother so that her child doesn't have to be taken into care, to giving a homeless man the deposit he needs to obtain a flat.

ASB Help is another charity which I founded. It aims to help people who have had to suffer anti-social behaviour, and it came about after I read of the appalling 2007 case of Fiona Pilkington from Leicester, who killed herself and her eighteen-year-old disabled daughter Francecca, after enduring several years of harassment and torment without the authorities doing anything to help. A national outcry ensued for a short while, but the problem has now been largely forgotten, except by the people who continue to suffer. Every week ASB Help gives practical and informed advice to thousands of people who feel powerless and ignored.

I then turned my attention to the injustices faced by those on zero-hour contracts. I readily acknowledge that some workers may be happy to accept them, but the fact remains that they have been unilaterally imposed on around 1 million people and that they can make life very difficult. If you don't know how many hours you will be working in any given week, how can you possibly budget your expenditure? How can you tell a potential landlord how much you will be earning? How can you organise, let alone afford to pay for, childcare if you may be sent home early because 'business is quiet'? How can you refuse a sexually exploitative boss demanding favours in return for work if hunger or eviction are the only alternatives? Only seven countries in the whole of the EU tolerate this aberration. We're one of them. I have therefore set up Zero Hours Justice to expose this ghastly practice and to lobby for change.

Having read Richard Brooks' fantastic books *The Great Tax Robbery* and *Bean Counters*, and spent some time with him, I also decided to campaign against aggressive tax avoidance. The team he and I helped to set up at TaxWatch (run by the brilliant George Turner) have investigated and published some really important exposés. Now they are working on a redefinition of tax avoidance and have put together an academic panel to quantify precisely how much tax the state is defrauded – otherwise known as the 'Tax Gap' – which, of course, could be put to better use to serve society.

CONCLUSION

My most recent project very much brings me back to the subject of this book: to encourage responsible capitalism. The Good Business Charter, set up with the support of both the CBI and the TUC, offers accreditation to organisations that meet ten specific criteria (real living wage, diversity and inclusion, etc.). With an annual charge of just £1 per employee per annum, it was launched on 1 February 2020, just a few weeks before lockdown in Britain. This may not have been the ideal time to start anything, but we have nevertheless had an amazing response from a range of businesses and charities large and small. Our outstanding CEO Jenny Herrera happens to both a chartered accountant and a practising Christian.

There are many social needs which could be addressed with the right kind of practical action, and I feel that anyone who can should take up the challenge and do something. It might be a local issue on your doorstep, or something particularly relevant to the business you own or work for.

I would also urge businesses to allocate a percentage of their profits to charity – and if they do that already, a larger percentage (Richer Sounds, the company I founded, gives away 15% of its profits). Then they should find charities to support where the money can make a real difference – not necessarily the large, household name charities, but ones that employees particularly care about and that may have a smaller or tighter focus.

So let's open our eyes to the reality and the limits of capitalism, make it more ethical where we can – and where we can't, use our skills, money and influence to help and protect the society which is so precious to us.

POSTSCRIPT

AFTER 40 YEARS I felt the time was right, if not exactly to hang up my boots, at least to start passing control of my business to the next generation. I had always been interested in the John Lewis Partnership model, and I also wanted to reward my wonderful colleagues in some way. Not having kids made both ambitions easier.

I first went public with my plan in November 2013 in an interview with the *Financial Times*, and was pleased to note that the following year, the then Chancellor, George Osborne, publicly encouraged business owners to create employee owner-ship trusts. In my case, I was able to give just under £4 million of the initial £9.2 million I received to my colleagues in the form of a personal one-off thank you gift of £1,000 (sadly, taxable) per person for each year of service they had given the company. Further payments will be made to me, assuming a continuing strong performance by the company.

When I announced the bonus to my colleagues at the Salvation Army Hall in Regent Street on Tuesday, 14 May 2019, you could have heard a pin drop. Then you could hear 150 senior colleagues asking each other, 'Did he say £10 for each year of service, or was it £100?' The money was put to good use, paying for everything from deposits on first homes to weddings to kitchens. And, if only for a few seconds, I would like to think that most of the people there loved me!

Who knows what the future will hold? For the moment, though, I am working hard to pass on my knowledge to the new generation at work and to pursue the social issues of the day that I feel strongly about.

ACKNOWLEDGEMENTS

A SMALL BUT exceptionally talented team helped me with this book – which was just as well!

Without the diligence and dedication of Kate Miller greatly assisting with the text and research there would be no book.

Nigel Wilcockson added his exceptional editing skills which have given my thinking another level of 'coherence'.

Teresa, my amazing PA of 25 years' standing, pulled everything together and kept everyone happy, as well as contributing her general wisdom throughout and checking the proofs for me.

My friend Paul Keenan encouraged me in the early stages, just as he did 25 years ago with my first book *The Richer Way*. He also introduced me to Richard Kilgarriff who acted as confidant, adviser and 'honorary' agent, and kindly escorted me to meet publishers.

Another close friend, Ian Grenfell, recommended that we be sure to visit Susan Sandon at Penguin Random House ... and the rest, as they say, is history.

Some really useful perspective was also provided by Niki Adams of the Crossroads Women's Centre in London, and by Richard Brooks, journalist and author of the excellent book *The Great Tax Robbery*.

And finally, my wonderful wife Rosie who is so supportive and encouraging of all my crazy ideas. She has helped me in everything I do – more than she knows.

Huge thanks to all of you very special people.

Julian Richer
York, 2018